Cracking the SAT French Subject Test

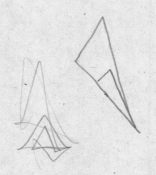

The Princeton Review

Cracking the SAT French Subject Test

By Monique Gaden and Simone Ingram

2005–2006 Edition

Random House, Inc.
New York

www.PrincetonReview.com

The Independent Education Consultants Association recognizes The Princeton Review as a valuable resource for high school and college students applying to college and graduate school.

Princeton Review Publishing, L.L.C.
2315 Broadway
New York, NY 10024
E-mail: booksupport@review.com

ISBN: 0-375-76449-6
ISSN: 1075-6051

Editor: Christiane Angeli
Production Editor: Patricia Dublin
Production Coordinator: Jennifer Arias

SAT is a registered trademark of the College Board.

Manufactured in the United States of America.

10 9 8 7 6 5 4 3 2

2005–2006 Edition

ACKNOWLEDGMENTS

Special thanks to Adam Robinson, who conceived of and perfected the Joe Bloggs approach to standardized tests and many of the other successful techniques used by The Princeton Review.

CONTENTS

Part I: Orientation   1

1   **Introduction**   3
2   **General Strategy**   9

Part II: Subject Review   13

3   **Vocabulary**   15
4   **Vocabulary Review**   35
5   **Grammar Review**   51
6   **Reading Comprehension**   103
7   **French Listening**   121

Part III: The Princeton Review Practice SAT French Subject Tests
        and Explanations   125

8   **Practice SAT French Subject Test 1**   127
9   **Practice SAT French Subject Test 1: Answers and Explanations**   147
10   **Practice SAT French Subject Test 2**   163
11   **Practice SAT French Subject Test 2: Answers and Explanations**   183

About the Authors   199

PART I

Orientation

1 Introduction

THE SAT SUBJECT TESTS

This book will give you all the tools you need to do your best on the SAT French Subject Test. Let's start with some general information.

WHAT ARE THE SAT SUBJECT TESTS?

They are a series of one-hour exams developed and administered by the Educational Testing Service (ETS) and the College Board. The SAT Subject Tests are designed to measure specific knowledge in specific areas. There are many different tests in many different subject areas, such as biology, history, French, and math. They are scored separately on a 200–800 scale.

HOW ARE SAT SUBJECT TESTS USED BY COLLEGE ADMISSIONS?

Because the tests are given in specific areas, colleges use them as another piece of admissions information and, often, to decide whether an applicant can be exempted from college requirements. A good SAT French score might place you in second-year French instead of first-year French, or exempt you from a foreign language requirement altogether.

SHOULD I TAKE THE SAT SUBJECT TESTS? HOW MANY? WHEN?

About one-third of the colleges that require SAT scores also require that you take two or three Subject Tests. Your first order of business is to start reading those college catalogs. College guidebooks, admissions offices, and guidance counselors should have this information as well.

As to which tests you should take, the answer is simple:

1. Those Subject Tests that you will do well on, and

2. The tests that the colleges you are applying to may require you to take.

The best possible situation, of course, is when the two match.

Some colleges have specific requirements, others do not. Again, start asking questions before you start taking tests. Once you find out which tests are required, if any, part of your decision making is done. The next step is to find out which of the tests will highlight your particular strengths.

Possibilities range from English literature, U.S. or world history, biology, chemistry, and physics to a variety of foreign languages.

As to when you should take the tests, schedule them as close as possible to the corresponding coursework you may be doing. If you plan to take the SAT Chemistry Subject Test, for example, and you are currently taking chemistry in high school, don't postpone the test until next year.

WHEN ARE THE SAT SUBJECT TESTS OFFERED?

In general, you can take from one to three Subject Tests per test date in October, November, December, January, May, and June at test sites across the country. Not all subjects are offered at each administration, so check the dates carefully.

How Do I Register for the Tests?

To register by mail, pick up a registration form and student bulletin at your guidance office. You can also register at the College Board website at www.collegeboard.com. This site contains other useful information such as the test dates and fees. If you have questions, you can talk to a representative at the College Board by calling 1-609-771-7600.

You may have your scores sent to you, to your school, and to four colleges of your choice. Additional reports will be sent to additional colleges for—you guessed it—additional money. The scores take about six weeks to arrive.

What's a Good Score?

That's hard to say, exactly. A good score is one that fits in the range of scores the college of your choice usually accepts or looks for. However, if your score falls below the normal score range for Podunk University, that doesn't mean you won't get into Podunk University. Schools are usually fairly flexible in what they are willing to look at as a "good" score for a particular student.

Along with your score, you will also receive a percentile rank. That number tells you how you fit in with the other test takers. In other words, a percentile rank of 60 means that 40 percent of the test takers scored above you and 60 percent scored below you.

What Is The Princeton Review?

The Princeton Review is a test-preparation company based in New York City. We have branches across the country and abroad. We've developed the techniques you'll find in our books, courses, and online resources by analyzing actual exams and testing their effectiveness with our students. What makes our techniques unique is that we base our principles on the same ones used by the people who write the tests. We don't want you to waste your time with superfluous information; we'll give you just the information you'll need to get great score improvements. You'll learn to recognize and comprehend the relatively small amount of information that's actually tested. You'll also learn to avoid common traps, to think like the test writers, to find answers to questions you're unsure of, and to budget your time effectively.

You need to do only two things: trust the techniques, and practice, practice, practice.

Is There Any Other Material Available for Practice?

Stay away from the plethora of other test-prep books available. The questions in the majority of books on the market bear little, if any, resemblance to actual SAT Subject Test questions. The College Board, however, publishes a book called *Real SAT Subject Tests*, which contains full-length tests in almost all the SAT subjects offered. You can also go to the College Board's website, www.collegeboard.com, for more information and practice questions.

After you've completed the practice tests and drills in this book, try out your new skills on real SAT Subject Test questions.

WHAT MAKES THIS BOOK DIFFERENT?

Most prep books for foreign language tests are written by academics who ramble on about the subtleties of the syntax of their chosen languages. Their cups runneth over with more rules and reasons about grammar than you could ever absorb in a limited period of time. Most of all, they take more interest in teaching you French with a capital F than in preparing you for the particular challenges of this test. Rather than waste your time—as other prep books do—rehashing every tedious rule of grammar, we'll cover only those points needed to get you a good score on the test. We want you to study effectively. What you do with your French on your own time is your business.

Some prep books can harm you more than help you by misleading you about the types of questions or by giving you so much to review that you don't know where to begin or what's most important. In our 20 years of test-prep experience, we've learned what you truly need to know to score your best.

WHAT IS THE SAT FRENCH SUBJECT TEST?

The SAT French is a 60-minute test with 85 to 90 questions designed to test whether you learned anything while studying French in high school.

WHAT DOES IT TEST?

The SAT French tests vocabulary, reading comprehension, and a few points of grammar. A strong vocabulary will help you score well on Vocabulary and Reading Comprehension. Our review groups words by category for easier recall and gives you tips for learning vocabulary.

As you probably know, French grammar is complex, but the SAT French Subject Test only tests you on a small portion of all grammar. You do not need to know spelling, where the accents go, or correct word order in a sentence. You don't need to know how to conjugate the *passé simple* or the imperfect of the subjunctive. We'll review only those points of grammar that serve you best on the test.

> You can't master all of the French language in a few weeks or even a month. Focus on the vocabulary and grammar that helps you on the test.

NOW FOR THE GOOD NEWS

In the scheme of standardized tests, the SAT French isn't all bad. Any standardized test provides you with a wealth of opportunity. Wouldn't you rather take a test in which you can use the Process of Elimination and guessing techniques than walk into a room and speak to a French person? By using an approach that has been developed over the years at The Princeton Review, you'll have the confidence and the ability to ace the SAT French Subject Test.

HOW IS THE SAT FRENCH SUBJECT TEST SCORED?

The scoring system for the SAT French is similar to that for the SAT. You are given a raw score based on the number of questions you got right minus one-third of a point for every wrong answer. The raw score is then converted to a scaled score ranging from 200 to 800.

> Your SAT French score may be used to place you into the appropriate level of French class in college. If you score well, you may be able to take fewer semesters of language class. If you score really well, you may be exempted from the language requirement completely.

How Will I Improve My Score?

Unfortunately, reading through this book may not be enough. It is important that you apply our techniques during the practice sections so that our approach will be second nature when you take the actual test.

Read one section of the book at a time and immediately apply what you have learned to the practice section that follows it. Then, read carefully through the explanations, looking for patterns in the mistakes that you made. If you notice that one type of question or topic is giving you trouble, go back and review the relevant section. Finally, before taking the diagnostic test at the back of the book, review both the general test-taking strategies and the specific question strategies. Again, after taking the test, notice where your mistakes were, and use that information to adjust your pacing and intensify your review.

This book is designed to help you focus on those points that will help you score higher. It assumes that you have a basic vocabulary in French and a rough grasp of grammar. The grammar section highlights the rules that are actually tested, giving you a concise explanation of each rule and examples of test questions. If you are someone who likes detailed explanations, you may want to have your school grammar book handy to use alongside this review book.

Although this book can be used alone, you may find it handy to have a French/English dictionary and a grammar book available as references while you read through the text. Don't use them on the practice tests, though!

For book updates, links to more information, and last-minute test changes, visit this book's Online Companion at www.PrincetonReview.com/cracking.

2

General Strategy

HOW TO IMPROVE

As on any multiple-choice standardized test, you can learn to leverage your knowledge into the best possible score by following a few simple principles.

ATTITUDE

Do not be intimidated by the test! This is only a test that stamps you with a number so that you can be easily classified by the colleges you apply to. It measures some vocabulary, some minor rules such as which phrases take the subjunctive, and, above all, how well you do on standardized tests.

We can't make up for what you did or didn't learn in school, but we can teach you to make the most of what you do know and boost your test-taking savvy. We'll teach you new ways of approaching the test: pacing yourself, spotting wrong answers, and using guessing skills that put you in control.

PACING

Standardized tests aren't like school tests. They are actually designed so that hardly anyone can finish all the questions. Don't stress about answering every question or getting through the entire test.

In school, most of us were trained to answer every question on a test. That made sense because those tests were usually written so that there was time to answer every question. On standardized tests, such thinking can lower your score. These tests are designed so that 99 percent of the population cannot finish the test without rushing and making careless mistakes. Slowing down—finding a pace at which you can work carefully and confidently—is the first step to improving your score. Remember, you are not given a negative score on a question you have left unanswered.

There is no advantage to answering all the questions on a test if you answer so hurriedly that you get most of them wrong. Think of each question as an investment in your score. Take enough time to make the work you put in pay off in terms of points. Most people don't realize that they can get a terrific score by doing fewer questions. While this philosophy holds true for all standardized tests, it is especially important for the SAT Subject Tests, in which one-third of a point is deducted for each wrong answer.

One caution: Working slowly and carefully is great. Spending five minutes to get an answer on a single question is not. Don't let your pride keep you struggling with a question that's giving you a hard time. Each question has the same value. Do what you can, eliminate wrong answer choices, and guess. Then move on to a new question.

You'll have one hour to work on the entire test. You are not timed on each section. That means you can spend less time on sections that you are stronger in, or just move at a steady, careful pace through the whole test.

WORK FOR ACCURACY, NOT FOR SPEED

The scoring system used by the College Board rewards you for slowing down. It is better to do fewer questions well than to do many questions badly.

The following guide tells you approximately how many questions you have to answer to get a particular score. (This is the approximate number you should answer—not counting guesses—making about five errors.) Keep in mind that the scale changes each year, depending on the difficulty of the exam.

To get this score:	Answer this many questions (out of 85):
400	10
450	20
500	25
550	35
600	45
650	55
700	65
750	75
800	85

So, to get a 600 you have to answer barely half of the test. You can skip the questions that give you the most trouble.

As you do each practice section, you can check your pacing by comparing the number you got right with the number you got wrong. If you made more than two careless errors in that section (not counting guesses), you may want to slow down and attempt fewer questions on the practice test.

You could skip as many as 20 questions and still score a 700.

WHICH ONES SHOULD YOU SKIP?

On Parts A and B, the questions are arranged roughly in order of increasing difficulty, so unless you are aiming for more than a 600, you may skip the last third of each part. On Parts C and D, there is no clear order of difficulty. Skip questions you don't like and spend time on those you do.

You don't have to answer the same proportion of questions on each part. For most people, reading comprehension is the most difficult and vocabulary is the easiest. If that's true for you, do extra vocabulary and fewer reading-comprehension questions.

Tailor your pacing strategy to your strengths and weaknesses. If your reading is good and your grammar is weak, pace yourself accordingly.

PROCESS OF ELIMINATION

No matter how good you are at French, you may still come across a question or two that will stump you. What can you do? Look for obviously incorrect answers, and get rid of them. It is often easier to find three wrong answers than it is to find one right one. If the sentence completion has something to do with going to the beach, an answer choice that means "pincushion" is probably not what you're looking for. The College Board also has some favorite ways to trap test takers who aren't completely sure of themselves. Once you know how they trick you, you're protected from falling into that trap and you're one answer choice closer to the correct one. On some occasions, you'll be able to eliminate all but the correct choice. If not, then:

Random vs. Educated Guessing

Make a distinction between random guessing and educated guessing. Random guessing (when you have no clue at all) won't help your score. Educated guessing (when you know enough to eliminate at least one answer choice) boosts your score.

Guess!

If you can eliminate even one answer choice, it's to your advantage to guess—you have a one-in-three chance of getting it right. If you're down to two choices and can't decide, guess and move on to the next question.

Aggressive guessing is what separates the great test taker from the average test taker. Guess once or twice and you may or may not help your score. Guess ten or more times, and by the law of averages, you'll be boosting your score.

You can also think of guessing as a way of getting partial credit for a question. The knowledge that lets you eliminate one or two answers increases your chances of getting full credit for the question.

OVERALL STRUCTURE OF THE TEST

The SAT French Subject Test consists of four types of questions. You are free to work on the sections or questions in any order that you choose. You will have 60 minutes to answer 85–90 questions.

The layout of each test will look something like this:

- Part A—Vocabulary Completions
  (approx. 20–26 questions)

- Part B—Grammar Blanks
  (approx. 15–20 questions)

- Part C—Paragraph Blanks
  (approx. 12–20 questions)

- Part D—Reading Comprehension
  (approx. 27 questions)

The exact breakdown of questions will vary from test to test. The list above gives you the approximate number of each type of question.

If Reading Comprehension contains "schedules and tickets" questions as well as traditional passages, then Reading Comprehension will have more questions and Grammar will have slightly fewer.

PART II

Subject Review

3
Vocabulary

PART A: VOCABULARY COMPLETIONS

Boost Your Vocab

Vocabulary questions make up more than a third of the test. The best way to boost your vocabulary is to read French on a regular basis. Keep your dictionary handy!

The first part of the test consists of approximately 20 to 26 vocabulary completions. Each question is a sentence containing a blank. Each of the four answer choices provides a word that could fill in the blank. The correct answer is the one that best completes the sentence in terms of the meaning of the word. (All choices will be grammatically correct.)

Here are the directions for this section as they appear on the test. Become familiar with these directions now so that you don't waste valuable time when you take the test.

Part A

Directions: This part consists of a number of incomplete statements, each having four suggested completions. Select the most appropriate completion and fill in the corresponding oval on the answer sheet.

The questions are arranged roughly in order of difficulty.

WHAT MAKES THE DIFFERENCE IN THIS SECTION?

If your vocabulary needs work, short, frequent study sessions will help you more than long, infrequent ones. Your brain will only be able to absorb a small amount of information at a time. Ten minutes a day between now and the test will make a big difference.

Vocabulary, vocabulary, vocabulary. If your vocabulary is not strong, start working on it right away. In Chapter 4, Vocabulary Review, there are several techniques designed to boost your vocabulary.

Test your vocabulary by writing the English translations of the following words.

Drill 1

Answers can be found on page 31.

une usine	a sponge x a factory
la honte	honesty x shame
l'oeuvre	discovery x the wor
en vouloir à	in want of x to be angry at
mou	soft
taquiner	tease
la foule	
ramasser	
soutenir	
repasser	

se méfier de _____

se débarrasser de _____

If you missed more than three of the words, you may need to give vocabulary work extra attention (Chapter 4).

IF YOU KNOW THE WORDS

FILL IN YOUR OWN WORD

As you read through the sentence, fill in your own word in English **before you look** at the answer choices.

> Le film était tellement amusant qu'elle . . . sans cesse.

If something is funny, what does someone do?

Now let's look at the answer choices and see which one is close to the English answer you decided on:

> (A) dansait
> (B) mangeait
> (C) riait
> (D) lisait

If you thought of the word "laughed" or "smiled," you can eliminate *dansait*, which means "danced," *mangeait*, which means "ate," and *lisait*, which means "read." The correct answer is *riait*, "laughed."

If you understand most of the words in the question, you'll have no problem filling in the blank.

Cover the answer choices and fill in a word for the following examples.

> Jean-Pierre a mal . . . parce qu'il a trop mangé.

> (A) à l'oreille
> (B) au ventre
> (C) aux genoux
> (D) à la tête

If someone ate too much, he would probably have a pain in the "belly." You could then eliminate (A), which means "the ear," (C), which means "the knees," and (D), which means "the head." Choice (B), meaning "the abdomen," is the correct answer.

> La banque se trouve . . . le supermarché et la poste.

> (A) dans
> (B) sur
> (C) pendant
> (D) entre

The word in the blank should give the position of the bank in relationship to the supermarket and the post office: "between" or "near." You can eliminate (A), which means "inside," (B), which means "on," and (C), which means "during." Choice (D), which means "between," is the correct answer.

Watch Out for Trap Answers

Don't immediately pick the first word that seems right. Look at all the answer choices, and leave in only those that might work. Then carefully compare the remaining choices before selecting an answer.

> Si tu n'as pas assez d'argent pour acheter le livre, tu peux le trouver à . . .
>
> (A) la librairie
> (B) l'épicerie
> (C) la bibliothèque
> (D) la papeterie

On average, each Part A section contains one question that tests your knowledge of body parts and one question that tests store names.

If you don't have enough money to buy a book, you will probably go to a "library." If you know the vocabulary, you might immediately identify the right answer. If not, eliminate (B), which means "grocery store," and (D), which means "stationery store." Is the answer *librairie* or *bibliothèque*? Which means "library"? The answer in this case is the less obvious one: (C), *bibliothèque*. *Librairie* means "bookstore." See page 50 for "Common Mix-Ups."

IF YOU DON'T KNOW ALL THE ANSWER CHOICES

Sometimes you'll be able to fill in a word, but you won't be sure which answer choice matches the word you picked. The following guessing techniques will improve your odds of picking the correct answer.

USE PROCESS OF ELIMINATION (POE)

First, clear out the deadwood. Eliminate answer choices that you are sure do not match the word you chose. With the remaining choices, try to guess what each means.

USE YOUR ENGLISH

Although it is your knowledge of French that is being tested, your own native language can often help you. Many English words are derived from French, so it makes sense that some words are nearly identical in both languages (but, again, watch out for these traps). How hard is it to guess what *régulier* means? *Transporter? Bière?*

Drill 2

Answers can be found on pages 31–32.

Decide what English words the following French words remind you of:

évaluer   _____

sacré   _____

retarder   _____

fréquenter   _____

nombre	_____
assurer	_____
raison	_____
plante	_____
attraper	_____
servir	_____
content	_____
accord	_____
cru	_____

Using English can help you make an educated guess about the meaning of a word. Based on that guess, you can decide to keep the word or eliminate it, narrowing the field of choices and improving your odds. Don't automatically pick the first word that reminds you of the English word you are looking for.

Use this technique with caution on difficult questions. On difficult questions (especially the last five questions), use this technique only to eliminate wrong choices, not to pick the right answer. On tough questions, if an answer choice reminds you strongly of the word you're looking for in English, it's practically guaranteed that it's a trap answer.

> If you understand how test writers think, you can get a question right even if you don't know the meaning of all the answer choices. On easy questions (the first third), the right answer will not be a tough vocabulary word. On hard questions (the final third), the right answer will not be the answer that reminds you of the word in English that you are looking for.

27. ------- des étudiants sortant de l'école a rompu le silence du quartier.

    (A) Le martelage
    (B) La chatière
    (C) Le ramassage
    (D) Le bavardage

This is a tough question. If you understand the sentence ("The ____ of the students leaving school broke the silence in the neighborhood."), you know you're looking for a word that means noise, talk, or chatter. Even if you weren't sure of the whole sentence, you might have seen "silence" and known that you were looking for a word that relates to silence. Which answer is a trap?

Choice (B) looks like the English word "chatter." Since this was a tough question (from the final third), you know it's a trap. *La chatière* actually means "the ventilation hole." The correct answer is (D), which means "the chatting." (A) means "the hammering" (*un marteau* is a hammer) and (C) means "the gathering of." On difficult questions, don't pick the answer that reminds you of the word you're looking for in English.

> On hard questions, be wary of trap answers but don't psych yourself out! If you know the meaning of all the words, the right answer is still the right answer. Don't cross off the right answer because you're afraid it's too "obvious." Trap answers have a specific feel to them.

LOOK FOR EASIER VERSIONS OF WORDS

On difficult questions (or if your vocabulary isn't very strong), you can sometimes figure out an easier version of the answer choices. For example, in the verb *feuilleter* you may see the word *feuille,* meaning "leaf" or "sheet of paper." Could there be a verb meaning "to leaf"? Yes, just as in English, you can "leaf" through a book.

What easier words do you see in the following words?

prochainement _____

emporter _____

parapluie _____

retarder _____

Well? In *prochainement,* you probably saw *prochain,* which means "next," so *prochainement* probably has something to do with being next. (It means "in a short while," or "coming up next.") You probably see *porter,* which means "to carry," in *emporter,* so you might be able to guess that *emporter* has a similar meaning. It means "to carry away." And what about *parapluie*? Recognize the word *pluie,* "rain"? So *parapluie* is likely to be "umbrella." *Retarder* has the word *tard,* or late, in it, so it's a safe bet that *retarder* means "to slow or delay."

AVOID LOOK-ALIKE ANSWERS

The College Board sometimes tries to trick you by providing answers that look like either the correct answer or a word that appeared in the sentence.

Je dois réparer ma montre, elle ne . . . plus.

(A) casse
(B) montre
(C) donne
(D) marche

If something needs to be fixed, what doesn't it do anymore? Probably, it doesn't work. Which answer choice means "to work"? Answer choice (B) is a look-alike trap here. *Montre,* meaning "show," is identical to the word *montre,* meaning "wristwatch," in the sentence. It's a trap! Eliminate it. The correct answer is (D) *marche.* The verb *marcher* used with an inanimate object means "to work or function correctly."

IF YOU DON'T UNDERSTAND THE SENTENCE

WORD ASSOCIATION

You often don't need the whole sentence to figure out what word you're looking for. Usually one or two key words in the sentence point to the answer.

Even if you're shaky on the exact meaning of the sentence, you can still make an educated guess for the answer. Go through the words in the sentence that you do know and see if any of the answer choices are in some way associated with those words.

For the following incomplete questions, pick the answer choice that makes the most sense given the words that are shown.

Drill 3
Answers can be found on pages 32–33.

xxxxxxxx xxxxxxxx xx légumes xxxx xxxxx . . .

vegetables

(A) cheminée
(B) jardin
(C) gazon
(D) quartier

xx xxxx xxxxxxx xx xxx *tombé* xxx xxxx . . .

fallen

(A) envolée
(B) échappée
(C) cassée
(D) attrapée

xx xx x xxx xxxxx xx *chaises* xxxx . . . xxxx xx xxxxx.

chairs

(A) assommer
(B) s'asseoir
(C) assurer
(D) associer

xxxxx xxxxxxxxx *ne se sent pas bien* xxxxx xxx xxxx x . . .

doesn't feel well

(A) de la fièvre
(B) une armoire
(C) un verger
(D) une annonce

xx xxxxx xxxx xxxxxxxxx xxxxx *mangé* xxx xxx . . .

eaten

(A) soutenir
(B) emporter
(C) avaler
(D) évaluer

SUMMARY

IF YOU KNOW ALL THE WORDS IN THE SENTENCE

- Fill in your own word in English.
- Eliminate obviously wrong answer choices.
- Examine remaining choices (avoid obvious traps).
- Pick your answer.

You probably have all kinds of French words stored in your memory. To help you on the test, you'll want to bring those words back to the surface. If you have a friend taking the test, practice speaking in French to each other a few minutes every day. Yes, you may feel silly, but it really will help. Also, check your TV or radio guides for programs in French, rent movies, and read websites in French.

If You Don't Know All the Answer Choices

- Use your English to eliminate wrong answers.
- Break words down into easy pieces to help you eliminate wrong answers.
- Guess.

If You Really Have No Clue At All

- Skip it and leave it blank.

If You're Not Sure of the Meaning of the Sentence

- Use word association.
- Guess.

PRACTICE SECTION

Part A

Directions: This part consists of a number of incomplete statements, each having four suggested completions. Select the most appropriate completion and fill in the corresponding oval on the answer sheet.

Answers can be found on pages 26–31.

1. Il fait froid dehors. Est-ce que toutes les . . . sont fermées?

   (A) chambres
   (B) cheminées
   (C) fenêtres
   (D) notes

2. Ne fais pas de bruit, les enfants sont . . .

   (A) venus
   (B) endormis
   (C) partis
   (D) tristes

3. Est-ce que ces fleurs sont de votre . . . ?

   (A) peinture
   (B) garage
   (C) jardin
   (D) verger

4. Ce manteau n'a pas de . . . où mettre mon porte-monnaie.

   (A) manches
   (B) portes
   (C) poches
   (D) monnaie

5. Jeanne s'est réveillée . . . pour voir le lever du soleil.

   (A) bas
   (B) haut
   (C) tard
   (D) tôt

6. Le train est parti . . . à midi.

   (A) du garage
   (B) du toit
   (C) de l'histoire
   (D) de la gare

7. Au repas du dimanche, nous mangeons un . . . avec des pommes de terre.

   (A) rôti
   (B) ruban
   (C) régime
   (D) rôle

8. Les tartes qui sont vendues dans cette . . . sont délicieuses.

   (A) pâtisserie
   (B) pharmacie
   (C) épicerie
   (D) librairie

9. Tu peux te laver maintenant. La salle de bains est . . .

   (A) gratuite
   (B) libre
   (C) livrée
   (D) seule

10. Mon . . . pour la classe est de traduire un poème de Rimbaud.

    (A) destin
    (B) doigt
    (C) droit
    (D) devoir

11. Le bruit dans un club peut être tellement fort qu'on a mal . . .

    (A) aux oreilles
    (B) aux orteils
    (C) à l'orgueil
    (D) à la gorge

12. La lune est si . . . que je ne peux pas imaginer que l'homme y est allé.

    (A) longue
    (B) fade
    (C) loin
    (D) immense

13. Ce n'est pas nécessaire de sortir la poubelle; Jean l'a . . . fait.

   (A) d'ici
   (B) dedans
   (C) déjà
   (D) d'un côté

14. Nous passerons Noël avec mes grands-parents . . .

   (A) cet été
   (B) cet automne
   (C) cet hiver
   (D) ce printemps

15. Vous avez déjà fait vos devoirs? Cela . . .

   (A) m'admet
   (B) me fait mal
   (C) me trompe
   (D) m'étonne

16. N'avez-vous pas . . . d'avoir fait cette bêtise?

   (A) courage
   (B) joie
   (C) hâte
   D) honte

17. Ce tissu est . . . comme la peau d'un bébé.

   (A) mouillé
   (B) nu
   (C) doux
   (D) cru

18. Le renard a . . . aux chasseurs.

   (A) ramassé
   (B) écrasé
   (C) échappé
   (D) couru

19. Le film commence à 8 heures exactement; soyez . . .

   (A) à l'heure
   (B) au courant
   (C) au loin
   (D) à présent

20. Il y a trop de monde ici; je préfère des cafés moins . . .

   (A) doués
   (B) chargés
   (C) tranquilles
   (D) fréquentés

21. Il n'y a pas assez de preuves pour . . . cet homme.

    (A) indiquer
    (B) inquiéter
    (C) insinuer
    (D) inculper

22. Mon frère est . . . ; il ne veut jamais m'aider à nettoyer la cuisine.

    (A) serviable
    (B) paresseux
    (C) redoutable
    (D) affolé

23. Le vase que j'ai laissé tomber s'est . . .

    (A) perdu
    (B) tricoté
    (C) évanoui
    (D) brisé

24. Vous pouvez trouver la robe de mariée de votre grand-mère si vous cherchez dans . . .

    (A) le plancher
    (B) le grenier
    (C) l'atelier
    (D) le magasin

25. Elle s'est débarrassée de ses vêtements . . .

    (A) désespérés
    (B) déprimés
    (C) abîmés
    (D) achetés

26. Diane s'est coupé les . . . pour être plus à la mode.

    (A) chevaux
    (B) chiffres
    (C) cheveux
    (D) chemins

27. Pour établir la validité de sa théorie, l'homme de science a fait . . .

    (A) un échec
    (B) une expérience
    (C) un résumé
    (D) un résultat

ANSWERS TO PRACTICE SECTION

1. It's cold outside. Are all the . . . closed?

   key phrase: *fait froid*
   fill in: windows

   (A) rooms
   (B) chimneys
   (C) windows
   (D) notes

2. Don't make any noise; the children are . . .

   key words: *bruit, enfants*
   fill in: asleep

   (A) arrived
   (B) asleep
   (C) gone
   (D) sad

3. Are these flowers from your . . . ?

   key word: *fleurs*
   fill in: garden

   (A) painting
   (B) garage
   (C) garden
   (D) orchard

4. This coat lacks . . . where I can put my wallet.

   key words: *manteau, porte-monnaie*
   fill in: pockets

   (A) sleeves
   (B) doors
   (C) pockets
   (D) money

5. Jeanne woke up . . . in order to see the sunrise.

   key phrase: *lever du soleil*
   fill in: early

   (A) low—*bas* like English "base"
   (B) high
   (C) late
   (D) early

6. The train left the . . . at noon.

   key word: *train*
   fill in: station

   (A) garage
   (B) roof
   (C) story
   (D) station

7. For Sunday's meal, we eat a . . . with potatoes.

   key word: *repas*
   fill in: food

   (A) roast—*rôti* like English "roast"
   (B) ribbon
   (C) diet
   (D) role, part

8. The tarts that are sold in this . . . are delicious.

   key word: *tartes*
   fill in: pastry shop

   (A) pastry shop
   (B) pharmacy
   (C) grocery store
   (D) bookstore

9. You can wash yourself now. The bathroom is . . .

   key phrase: *salle de bains*
   fill in: free, open, empty

   (A) free (no cost)
   (B) free (not occupied)
   (C) delivered
   (D) alone—*seule* like English "solo"

10. My . . . for class is to translate a poem of Rimbaud's.

    key word: *classe*
    fill in: homework, assignment

    (A) destiny—*destin* like English
    (B) finger
    (C) right
    (D) homework

11. The noise in a club can be so loud that it hurts one's . . .

key word: *bruit*
fill in: ears

(A) ears
(B) toes—*orteils* is a misleading look-alike
(C) pride
(D) throat

12. The moon is so . . . that I cannot imagine that man has gone there.

key word: *lune*
fill in: far away

(A) long—*longue* like English
(B) bland
(C) far
(D) immense—*immense* like English

13. It's not necessary to take out the garbage; Jean did it . . .

key words: *l'a . . . fait*
fill in: already

(A) from here
(B) inside
(C) already
(D) from one side

14. We are spending Christmas with my grandparents . . .

key word: *Noël*
fill in: winter

(A) this summer
(B) this autumn—*automne* like English
(C) this winter
(D) this spring

15. You've already done your homework? That . . .

key word: *déjà*
fill in: surprises me, pleases me

(A) admits me
(B) hurts me
(C) fools me
(D) surprises me

16. Aren't you . . . of doing that stupid thing?

key word: *bêtise*
fill in: ashamed, embarrassed

(A) courageous—*courage* like English
(B) joyful—*joie* like English
(C) haste
(D) ashamed

17. This fabric is . . . like the skin of a baby.

key phrase: *peau d'un bébé*
fill in: soft

(A) wet
(B) nude—*nu* like English
(C) soft
(D) crude—*cru* like English

18. The fox . . . the hunters.

key words: *renard, chasseurs*
fill in: escaped, was caught

(A) collected
(B) crushed
(C) escaped
(D) ran

19. The film starts at exactly
8 o'clock; be . . .

key word: *commence*
fill in: on time, early

(A) on time
(B) up to date
(C) from afar
(D) at the present time

20. There are too many people here; I prefer cafés that
are less . . .

key phrase: *trop de monde*
fill in: crowded

(A) gifted
(B) loaded
(C) quiet—*tranquilles* like English
(D) popular—where people go frequently

21. There is not enough evidence . . . this man.

    key phrase: *pas assez de preuves*
    fill in: to convict, charge, indict

    (A) to indicate
    (B) to worry
    (C) to insinuate
    (D) to indict

22. My brother is . . .; he never wants to help me clean the kitchen.

    key phrase: *il ne veut jamais m'aider*
    fill in: lazy, selfish

    (A) helpful
    (B) lazy
    (C) formidable
    (D) panic-stricken— *folie* like English "folly"

23. The vase that I dropped . . .

    key phrase: *laissé tomber*
    fill in: broke, shattered

    (A) is lost
    (B) is knit
    (C) fainted
    (D) broke, shattered

24. You can find your grandmother's wedding dress if you look in . . .

    key phrase: *la robe de mariée de votre grand-mère*
    fill in: the attic

    (A) the floor
    (B) the attic
    (C) the studio
    (D) the store

25. She got rid of her . . . clothing.

    key phrase: *s'est débarrassée*
    fill in: unwanted, messed up

    (A) hopeless
    (B) depressed
    (C) torn, worn
    (D) bought

26. Diane cut her . . . so she would be more fashionable.

key phrase: *s'est coupé*
fill in: hair

 (A) horses—misleading look-alike: *chevaux* for
   cheveux
 (B) numbers
 (C) hair
 (D) paths

27. To establish the validity of his theory, the scientist
 conducted . . .

key phrase: *établir la validité*
fill in: an experiment, study

 (A) a failure
 (B) an experiment
 (C) a summary
 (D) a result

ANSWERS TO DRILLS

Drill 1 (page 16)

une usine	a factory
la honte	shame
l'œuvre	the work
en vouloir à	to be angry at, to have a grudge against
mou	soft
taquiner	to tease
la foule	the crowd
ramasser	to gather, to pick up
soutenir	to support, to sustain
repasser	to pass by again, to iron
se méfier de	to mistrust
se débarrasser de	to get rid of

Drill 2 (page 18)

évaluer	to evaluate
sacré	sacred
retarder	to delay, to slow down
fréquenter	to go somewhere frequently, to see someone on a regular basis
nombre	number
assurer	to assure
raison	reason
plante	plant
attraper	to catch, to trap
servir	to serve

content	content or happy
accord	accord or harmony
cru	crude or raw

Drill 3 (page 21)

xxxx xxxx xxxxxxxx xx *légumes* xxxx xxxxx . . .

vegetables

(A) *cheminée*
chimney
(B) *jardin*
garden
(C) *gazon*
lawn
(D) *quartier*
quarter or neighborhood

xx xxxx xxxxxxx xx xxx *tombé* xxx xxxx . . .

fallen

(A) *envolée*
taken flight
(B) *échappée*
escaped
(C) *cassée*
broken
(D) *attrapée*
caught

xx xx x xxx xxxxx xx *chaises* xxxx . . . xxxx xx xxxxx.

chairs

(A) *assommer*
to knock out
(B) *s'asseoir*
to sit down
(C) *assurer*
to assure
(D) *associer*
to associate

xxxxx xxxxxxxxx *ne se sent pas bien* xxxxx xxx xxxx x . . .

doesn't feel well

(A) *de la fièvre*
a fever
(B) *une armoire*
a wardrobe
(C) *un verger*
an orchard
(D) *une annonce*
an announcement

xx xxxxx xxxx xxxxxxxxx xxxxx *mangé* xxx xxx . . .

                                    eaten

(A) *soutenir*
     to support
(B) *emporter*
     to take or carry away
(C) *avaler*
     to swallow
(D) *évaluer*
     to evaluate

4

Vocabulary Review

HOW TO IMPROVE YOUR VOCABULARY

The following vocabulary list organizes words in logical categories. This will make memorizing easier. Look through each category and concentrate on the words you don't know. If your vocabulary is already pretty good, concentrate on the most difficult words, which appear at the end of each category.

If you really want to imprint these words on your brain, passive reading is not enough. Try one or more of the following techniques to increase your learning.

FLASH CARDS

The old favorite. Put the French word on one side, the English on the other. If you want to get fancy, color-code by category or make up a symbol. This way you can mix up words in any order. On the French side, include part of speech, gender, and a sentence. Whenever you have a few minutes, pull out your cards and test yourself.

MNEMONICS

If it works for you, think of a funny image or sound that corresponds to the word. The more outrageous, the easier it will be to remember. Make up your own mnemonics and add them to your flash cards.

POSTERS

Make a list of words and definitions and hang them on your wall. As you go about your business, glance at the poster and review a few words.

These are only a few of the ways you can work on your vocabulary. Anything you do to make it more creative or colorful (literally—use colored pens, colored index cards, stickers, or markers) will increase your ability to learn and remember vocabulary.

VOCABULARY LIST

LE TEMPS	TIME
Une année	**A year**
un an	a year (always used for age)
une année	a year (as in *l'année dernière*, last year)
un mois	a month
une semaine	a week
un jour	a day
une journée	a day (as in *toute la journée*, all day long)
un calendrier	a calendar
un horaire	a schedule

Un An vs. Une Année

What's the difference between *un an* and *une année*? It's subtle. *Un an* is a unit of time. For example, "*J'ai passé deux ans à Paris.*" *Une année* is used when describing not the unit, but the full span of time. For example, "*l'année que j'ai passée en France.*"

Un jour	A day
le matin	the morning
la matinée	the morning
midi	noon
l'après-midi (masc. or fem.)	the afternoon
le soir	the evening
la soirée	the evening
la nuit	the night
minuit	midnight
l'aube (fem.)	daybreak
l'aurore (fem.)	dawn
le crépuscule	twilight
le lever du soleil	the sunrise
le coucher du soleil	the sunset

Une heure	An hour
une minute	a minute
une seconde	a second
un moment	a moment
un instant!	just a moment!
une montre	a watch
un réveil	an alarm clock
une horloge	a clock

Expressions de temps	Expressions of time
être à l'heure	to be on time
être en retard	to be late
être en avance	to be ahead of schedule
tôt	early
tard	late
avant	before
après	after
arriver de bonne heure	to arrive early
déjà	already
bientôt	soon
prochainement	shortly
toujours	always

jamais	never
longtemps	for a long time
régulièrement	regularly
se dépêcher	to hurry
se précipiter	to rush

Les vacances (fem.) — Holidays

un jour férié	a holiday
un jour de congé	a day off
être en vacances	to be on vacation
faire la grasse matinée	to sleep late

The expression *"faire la grasse matinée"* means *"se lever très tard."*

Les saisons (fem.) — Seasons

le printemps	spring
l'été (masc.)	summer
l'automne (masc.)	autumn, fall
l'hiver (masc.)	winter

LA NATURE — NATURE

Le temps qu'il fait — Weather conditions

le soleil	the sun, the sunshine
être bronzé	to be tanned
quel temps fait-il?	what's the weather like?
il fait du soleil	the sun is shining
il fait beau	the weather is nice
il fait chaud	it is hot
par beau temps	in good weather
le nuage	the cloud
il pleut	it is raining
un parapluie	an umbrella
être trempé	to be soaked
il fait mauvais	the weather is bad
par mauvais temps	in bad weather
la neige	the snow
il neige	it is snowing
il fait froid	it is cold

Pleurer vs. *Pleuvoir*
A common mistake is to mix up *"pleurer"* (to cry) and *"pleuvoir"* (to rain).

Le plein air

dehors	outside
un arbre	a tree
une branche	a branch
une feuille	a leaf
un verger	an orchard
récolter	to harvest
ramasser	to gather, to pick up
le jardin	the garden
le gazon	the lawn
une fleur	a flower
une plante	a plant
la poussière	the dust
se promener	to take a walk

The outdoors

La Maison

le toit	the roof
la cheminée	the chimney, the fireplace
une fenêtre	a window
ouvrir	to open
fermer	to close
en haut	upstairs
la salle de bains	the bathroom
se laver	to wash (oneself)
la baignoire	the bathtub
prendre un bain	to take a bath
la douche	the shower
prendre une douche, se doucher	to take a shower
la chambre à coucher	the bedroom
un meuble	a piece of furniture
frotter	to rub
astiquer	to polish
le lit	the bed

The Home

la chaise	the chair
le fauteuil	the armchair
s'asseoir	to sit down
se coucher	to go to bed
s'endormir	to fall asleep
se réveiller	to wake up
se lever	to get up
l'oreiller (masc.)	the pillow
le matelas	the mattress
les couvertures (fem.)	the blankets, the covers
en bas	downstairs
la salle à manger	the dining room
la cuisine	the kitchen
le four	the oven
la cuisinière	the stove, the cook (fem.)
le cuisinier	the cook (masc.)
le grenier	the attic
l'atelier (masc.)	the studio, the workshop

This Should "Cover" It

Other common mix-ups are "*les couvertures*" (the blankets), "*le couvert*" (the table setting or cover charge), and "*le couvercle*" (the lid).

EN VILLE (FEM.)   IN TOWN

l'immeuble (masc.)	the building
le gratte-ciel	the skyscraper
le trottoir	the sidewalk
la zone piétonne	the pedestrian zone
le quartier	the neighborhood
la banlieue	the suburb
habiter dans les environs de	to live on the outskirts of
habiter en banlieue	to live in the suburbs

Les courses (fem.)   Shopping

la boulangerie	the bakery
le boulanger	the baker
le pain	the bread
le croissant	the croissant (crescent roll)
la pâtisserie	the pastry shop, the pastry

le pâtissier	the pastry cook
les pâtisseries (fem.)	pastries
une tarte	a tart
un gâteau	a cake
un petit gâteau	a cookie
un biscuit salé	a cracker
un éclair	an éclair, a flash of lightning
les pâtes	pasta
l'épicerie (fem.)	the grocery store
l'épicier (masc.)	the grocer
les légumes (masc.)	the vegetables
les fruits (masc.)	the fruits
une pomme	an apple
une orange	an orange
les raisins	grapes
les raisins secs	raisins
un concombre	a cucumber
les pommes de terre	potatoes
le fromage	cheese
la fromagerie	the cheese store
la boucherie	the butcher shop
le boucher	the butcher
la viande	meat
un rôti	a roast
livrer	to deliver
vendre	to sell
acheter	to buy
faire les courses	to go shopping, to run errands
un besoin	a need
avoir besoin de	to need
l'argent (masc.)	money
retirer de l'argent	to withdraw money
le repas	the meal
le déjeuner	lunch

le dîner	dinner
une bière	a beer
le vin	wine
une papeterie	a stationery store
une librairie	a bookstore
un tabac	a café that sells tobacco items

Au Restaurant (Masc.) — At the Restaurant

un restaurant	a restaurant
fréquenter	to go to a place frequently
fréquenté	crowded, popular
un garçon, un serveur	a waiter
une serveuse	a waitress
un pourboire	a tip
l'addition (fem.)	the bill, the check
le couvert	the table setting, the cover charge
mettre le couvert	to set the table
débarrasser la table	to clear the table
se débarrasser de	to get rid of
une cuillère	a spoon
un couteau	a knife
une fourchette	a fork
une assiette	a plate
le verre	the glass
remplir	to fill
avaler	to swallow
servir	to serve
se servir de	to use, to help oneself
la recette	the recipe
une boulette de viande	a meatball
mou/molle	soft
cru/crue	raw
cuit/cuite	cooked
saignant/saignante	rare
gras/grasse	greasy, fatty

LES PROFESSIONS (FEM.)

un docteur	a doctor
un médecin	a physician
un avocat	a lawyer, an avocado
un professeur	a teacher, a professor
un(e) étudiant(e)	a student
un(e) journaliste	a journalist
un chanteur/une chanteuse	a singer
un acteur/une actrice	an actor, an actress
un metteur en scène	a director, a producer
une oeuvre	a work
un chef-d'oeuvre	a masterpiece
l'informatique (fem.)	computer science
un ordinateur	a computer
la facture	the bill, the invoice
l'usine (fem.)	the factory
l'outil (masc.)	the tool

PROFESSIONS

LE CORPS HUMAIN

la tête	the head
la figure, le visage	the face
l'oeil/les yeux (masc.)	the eye/the eyes
le nez	the nose
la bouche	the mouth
la lèvre	the lip
la dent	the tooth
la langue	the tongue
une oreille	an ear
le cou	the neck
se faire mal à l'épaule	to hurt one's shoulder
une épaule	a shoulder
la poitrine	the chest
un bras	an arm
la main	the hand
un doigt	a finger
un coude	an elbow

THE HUMAN BODY

un ongle	a nail
le poignet	the wrist
la hanche	the hip
une jambe	a leg
un genou	a knee
les cheveux	hair
un poumon	a lung
le rein	the kidney
un orteil	a toe
le dos	the back
transpirer	to sweat
gros	fat
mince	slim, thin
maigre	skinny

LES VÊTEMENTS (MASC.)   CLOTHES

une robe	a dress
une chemise	a shirt
un tailleur	a woman's suit
un costume	a man's suit
une jupe	a skirt
un manteau	a coat
un imperméable	a raincoat
une chaussure/un soulier	a shoe
une botte	a boot
une chaussette	a sock
un pantalon	a pair of pants
une manche	a sleeve
une ceinture	a belt
une poche	a pocket
la cravate	the tie
le repassage	the ironing
un fil	a thread
une aiguille	a needle
la taille	the size, the waist

LES VOYAGES (MASC.)

TRAVEL

un voyage	a trip
le vélo, la bicyclette	the bicycle
la voiture	the car, the carriage, the wagon
une autoroute	a highway
rouler	to move forward, to roll
l'essence	gas
avoir une panne d'essence	to run out of gas
une roue	a wheel
un pneu	a tire
la station-service	the gas station, the repair garage
s'arrêter	to stop
reculer	to back up
le train	the train
la gare	the train station
demander un renseignement	to ask for information
un bateau	a boat
une croisière	a cruise
un avion	a plane
atterrir	to land
l'atterrissage	the landing
voler	to fly
un vol	a flight
la valise	the suitcase
le billet	the ticket
l'agence de voyages (fem.)	the travel agency
traverser	to cross
transporter	to transport
emporter	to carry away
proche	near
loin	far
le décalage horaire	the time difference, the jet lag

UN ACCIDENT

AN ACCIDENT

le dégât	the damage

la faute	the fault, the mistake
grave	serious
le témoin	the witness
être témoin de	to witness
renverser quelqu'un	to hit somebody
soutenir	to hold up, to support
secourir, aider	to help
sauver	to save
au secours!	help!
avoir tort	to be wrong
avoir raison	to be right
échapper	to escape
attraper	to catch
éviter	to avoid
blesser	to injure
une blessure	an injury
assommer	to knock down
l'assurance (fem.)	the insurance
assurer	to insure, to assure
arrêter	to stop, to arrest
la prison	the jail
enfermer	to lock up

"Help!"
You call for help in French by yelling *"Au secours!"*

LA MALADIE — ILLNESS

un rhume	a cold
être enrhumé	to have a cold
avoir de la fièvre	to have a fever
avoir la grippe	to have the flu
malade	sick, ill
la douleur	the pain
s'évanouir	to faint
avoir mal à la gorge	to have a sore throat
avoir mal à la tête	to have a headache
le traitement	the treatment

L'ÉMOTION (FEM.)

	EMOTION
joyeux/joyeuse	joyful
heureux/heureuse	happy
content/contente	glad, pleased, happy, content
fier/fière	proud
la confiance	confidence or trust
le plaisir	the pleasure
comblé	fortunate, happy
combler	to fill up
l'accord (masc.)	the agreement
être d'accord	to agree
l'agrément (masc.)	the pleasure, the approval
savant	learned, knowledgeable
sage	wise
profond	profound or deep
étonner	to astonish
s'étonner	to be amazed by
estimer	to hold in esteem, to estimate
tolérer	to tolerate
surprendre	to surprise
avoir hâte de	to be eager to, to be impatient to
méchant	mean, nasty
malheureux	unhappy
en colère, fâché	angry
tromper	to trick, to deceive
s'ennuyer	to be bored
ennuyeux/ennuyeuse	boring
énervé	edgy
j'en ai marre, j'en ai ras le bol	I am fed up, I have had enough
taquiner	to tease
la honte	shame
avoir honte de	to be ashamed of
honteux	shameful, ashamed

"Congrats!"
You congratulate someone in French by saying "*Félicitations!*"

A great idiom (very colloquial) for expressing frustration is *J'en ai ras le bol!*, which means roughly, "I've had it up to here!"

méfiance	mistrust
se méfier de	to distrust
triste	sad
avoir de la peine	to be sad
faire de la peine	to hurt someone's feelings
en vouloir à	to be angry at, to have a grudge against
bassement	meanly
je m'en doute	I suspect it, I can imagine

LES NOMBRES (MASC.)   NUMBERS

le numéro	the number
le nombre	the number as in quantity
le compte	the count, the account
la somme	the sum
les chiffres	figures, numerals, digits
beaucoup	a lot
peu	little or few
plus	more
moins	less or fewer
évaluer	to evaluate
l'augmentation (fem.)	the increase
la croissance	the growth
la subvention	the subsidy
le manque	the lack
un tas de choses	many things
rien	nothing
tout	everything
la foule	the crowd

L'ÉCOLE (FEM.)   SCHOOL

une bourse d'études	a scholarship
feuilleter	to leaf through
permettre	to permit, to allow
traduire	to translate

enseigner	to teach
parler couramment	to speak fluently
une dissertation	an essay, a paper
admettre	to admit
félicitations!	congratulations!
souligner	to underline
une bonne note	a good grade
une erreur	a mistake
se tromper	to make a mistake
constater une erreur	to discover a mistake
un débouché	an opening, an outlet

The French school system is quite different from ours. By high school (*le lycée*), students have been divided into categories, each of which has a learning specialty: sciences, languages, economics, literature, etc. At the end of *le lycée*, students must pass a comprehensive exam, *le baccalauréat (le bac)*, to graduate.

LES SPORTS (MASC.) SPORTS

entraîner	to train, to coach
s'entraîner	to practice, to train
l'entraînement (masc.)	practice, training
une course	a race
tenter	to attempt, to tempt
atteindre	to reach
un but	a goal
étendre le bras	to stretch out one's arm
accomplir	to achieve
un exploit	a feat
souple	flexible
s'assouplir	to limber up, to become supple
repousser	to push back
monter	to go up
escalader, grimper	to climb
le football	soccer

Les Faux Amis		Common Mix-Ups	
la librairie	bookstore	**and** *la bibliothèque*	the library
la gare	the train station	**and** *la station service*	the gas station
le billet	the ticket	**and** *la facture*	the bill
crier	to shout, to scream	**and** *pleurer*	to cry
une course	an errand	**and** *un cours* *une classe*	a class, a course of study
une course	a race	**and** la race	the race, the ethnicity
le couvert	the table setting, the cover charge	**and** *la couverture*	the cover, the blanket
blesser	to wound, to hurt	**and** *bénir*	to bless
l'éditeur	the publisher	**and** *le rédacteur*	the editor
le spectacle	the show, the play	**and** *les lunettes*	the eyeglasses
l'agrément	the pleasure, the approval	**and** *l'accord*	the agreement
le stage	the training course, the internship	**and** *la scène*	the stage
la droguerie	hardware store	**and** *la pharmacie*	drugstore
déranger	to disturb	**and** *détraquer*	to derange or unsettle
passer un examen	to take an exam	**and** *réussir un examen*	to pass an exam

Only two or three of the questions on Part A will have tricky mix-ups.

Vocabulary questions on Part C will often have mix-ups. Usually you will be given four words that are close in meaning or look alike.

French words that look and sound similar but have different meanings

pleurer	to cry	*pleuvoir*	to rain
tromper	to deceive	*tremper*	to soak
vouloir	to want	*en vouloir à*	to be angry at
douter	to doubt	*se douter de*	to suspect

5

Grammar Review

Grammar is tested on both Parts B and C of the SAT French Subject Test. **Part B tests only grammar**, while **Part C tests both grammar and vocabulary**. The same points of grammar are tested on both B and C. As we explained before, the grammar tested on the SAT French is a very small area of French grammar. This chapter will explain exactly what you need to know. But first, here's a point-by-point summary of the question types you can expect.

PART B: GRAMMAR

Part B will consist of approximately 15 to 20 questions, placed in order of difficulty. The first third of the questions will be easy, the next third will be of intermediate difficulty, and the last seven questions will be difficult.

In these questions, there will be a sentence with a blank. You will choose the answer that is grammatically correct.

Become familiar with these directions that appear on the real test:

Part B

<u>Directions:</u> Each of the following sentences contains a blank. From the four choices given, select the one that can be inserted in the blank to form a grammatically correct sentence and fill in the corresponding oval on the answer sheet. Choice (A) may consist of dashes that indicate that no insertion is required to form a grammatically correct sentence.

Jean-Claude est venu avec -------.

(A) ils
(B) leur
(C) eux
(D) soi

The correct answer is (C).

PART C: COMPLETE THE PARAGRAPH

Part C tests both grammar and vocabulary. In this section, there are approximately 12 questions in no clear order of difficulty.

On this part, several questions are combined in one paragraph. You may have three or four mini-paragraphs with three to five blanks within each, or you may have one long paragraph. You are asked to select the answers that best complete the sentences on the basis of either vocabulary or grammar.

Become familiar with these directions:

Part C

Directions: The paragraphs below contain blank spaces indicating omissions in the text. For some blanks it is necessary to choose the completion that is most appropriate to the meaning of the passage; for other blanks, to choose the one completion that forms a grammatically correct sentence. In some instances, choice (A) may consist of dashes that indicate that no insertion is required to form a grammatically correct sentence. In each case, indicate your answer by filling in the corresponding oval on the answer sheet. Be sure to read each paragraph completely before answering the questions related to it.

This section combines the characteristics of parts A and B. The same grammar is tested on both parts. The small differences between the two are discussed at the end of this chapter.

KNOW WHAT YOU ARE LOOKING FOR

All the grammar questions on the SAT French Subject Test will fall into one of the following four categories.

1.   Pronouns

2.   Verbs

3.   Prepositions

4.   Odds and ends

The best way to improve in these areas is to learn the grammatical rules that are tested again and again. These rules are covered in the following grammar review.

GRAMMAR REVIEW

This is a great section for improvement. Why? Because to do well on the grammar review you need to review only a limited number of rules. Those rules will lead you to the right answer again and again. Unlike vocabulary, where luck determines whether the words you've learned will show up, grammar rules—and therefore, the content of these test questions—stay the same.

Good news: Only a minuscule number of grammar questions (around two) will test you on whether a noun is masculine or feminine.

You'll be tested primarily on three things: pronouns, verbs, and prepositions. Each question will address only one grammatical point. We'll cover each of these categories, giving you the rules that get you right answers. We'll also give practice questions for each category. Finally, we'll cover some odds and ends that occasionally show up on the test.

BASIC TERMS

You won't be tested on this material, but take a quick look through to make sure that you understand what the following terms mean. We'll be using them in this grammar review.

PARTS OF SPEECH

1. **Noun**—a person, place, thing, quality, or action. It can be either a subject or an object.

2. **Verb**—the action that is being performed by the subject

3. **Pronoun**—a word that takes the place of a noun

4. **Preposition**—a word that expresses the relationship of one word to another in terms of direction, motion, or position

5. **Adjective**—a descriptive word that gives more information about a noun

6. **Adverb**—a word that modifies a verb, an adjective, or another adverb

7. **Article**—a small word that gives a little information about a noun

None of this terminology is needed for the test. Understanding these terms, however, will help you understand the explanations in the grammar review that follows.

SENTENCE STRUCTURE

1. **Subject**—the person or thing in the sentence that is performing the action

2. **Compound subject**—two nouns or pronouns performing the action together

3. **Object**—the person or thing that is on the receiving end of the action

4. **Direct object**—an object that doesn't need a preposition to be the object

5. **Indirect object**—an object that needs a preposition in order to serve as the object

6. **Infinitive**—the form of a verb that uses "to," as in "to go" or "to speak"

7. **Auxiliary verb**—in the past tense, a helper verb that comes before the past participle

8. **Past participle**—in the past tense, the form of the verb that teams up with the auxiliary or "helper" verb

Joe and Ellen	have worked	hard	for	their	promotions.
compound subject	aux. verb + past participle	adverb	preposition	possessive adjective	indirect object
They	baked	a	delicious	cake.	
subject pronoun	verb	article	adjective	direct object	

PRONOUNS

A quarter of all grammar questions on the SAT French will test you on your knowledge of pronouns. Unlike English, which uses mainly two basic forms of pronouns (he and him, for example), French uses four important forms of pronouns: subject pronouns, direct object pronouns, indirect object pronouns, and stressed pronouns.

WHAT IS A PRONOUN?

A pronoun takes the place of a noun. It stands in for the full name or description of a person, place, or thing. In French, a pronoun will take different forms depending on what type of noun it replaces. Half of the pronoun questions on the test ask you to choose among subject pronouns, direct or indirect object pronouns, and stressed pronouns.

1. SUBJECT PRONOUNS

Subject pronouns replace the subject of the sentence.

> **Jean** *a montré son dessin à Edith.*
> **Jean** showed his drawing to Edith.

> ***Il*** *a montré son dessin à Edith.*
> **He** showed his drawing to Edith.

je or *j'*	=	I	*nous* =	we
tu	=	you	*vous* =	you (plural or formal singular)
il	=	he	*ils* =	they (masculine)
elle	=	she	*elles* =	they (feminine)

The subject pronoun *ils* (plural, masculine) is used both for groups of men only (or boys) and for groups of men and women, even if there are more women than men in the group. Hmmm.

These pronouns are usually the wrong answer choices. Why? Because these are the pronouns with which everyone is most familiar and comfortable.

2. Direct Object Pronouns

These pronouns replace the direct object of a sentence. The direct object answers the question "what?"

> *Jean a montré **son dessin** à Edith.*
>> Jean showed **his drawing** to Edith.

> *Jean **l'a** montré à Edith.*
>> Jean showed **it** (the drawing) to Edith.
>
> Notice that the direct object pronoun is placed before the verb.

When a direct object pronoun comes before a verb that starts with a vowel, the vowel in the pronoun is dropped and replaced with an apostrophe. For example, *me* becomes *m'* and *le* or *la* becomes *l'*.

me or *m'* =	me	*nous*	=	us
te or *t'* =	you	*vous*	=	you (plural or formal)
le or *l'* =	him or it	*les*	=	them (person or thing both masculine and feminine)
la or *l'* =	her or it			

3. Indirect Object Pronouns

These pronouns replace the indirect object of a sentence. The indirect object answers the questions "to what?" or "to whom?" Notice that the pronoun replaces both the indirect object and the preposition that goes with it.

> *Jean a montré son dessin **à Edith**.*
>> Jean showed his drawing **to Edith**.

> *Jean **lui** a montré son dessin.*
>> Jean showed **her** his drawing.

Notice also that the indirect object pronoun is placed before the verb.

me or *m'* =	me	*nous*	=	us
te or *t'* =	you	*vous*	=	you (plural or formal)
lui =	to him or her	*leur*	=	to them

4. STRESSED PRONOUNS

Stressed pronouns have no real English equivalent. In French, they are used as the object of certain prepositions and in compound subjects or objects.

moi	=	me or I	*nous*	=	us or we
toi	=	you	*vous*	=	you (plural or formal)
lui	=	him or he	*eux*	=	them or they (masculine or including both masculine and feminine)
elle	=	her or she	*elles*	=	them or they (feminine)

Use a stressed pronoun

1. As the object of a preposition (*à, avec, chez, sans*) following the verb.

   *Je suis allé au restaurant **avec mes amis**.*
   > I went to the restaurant with my friends.

   *Je suis allé au restaurant **avec eux**.*
   > I went to the restaurant with them.

   Notice that the pronoun replaces the indirect object but not the preposition that goes with it.

   > If you are asked to put a pronoun directly after a preposition (*à, chez*), you must use the stressed form of the pronoun.

2. **With the expression** *c'est. . . qui* or *que. . .* or *ce sont. . . qui* or *que. . . .*

   *C'est ma soeur **qui** a gagné la course.*
   > It is my sister who won the race.

   *C'est **elle** qui a gagné la course.*
   > She won the race.

   *Ce sont les livres **que** je veux.*
   > These are the books I want.

   *Ce sont **eux** que je veux.*
   > They are the ones I want.

3. **In a sentence in which the verb is dropped.**

   *Qui a fait cela? (C'est) **moi**.*
   > Who did this? I did.

Hey You!

If a command is being given and the object pronoun (either direct or indirect) is first person singular, it changes from the usual *me* to *moi*. For example:

Pouvez-vous me téléphoner?   *Téléphonez-moi!*
    Can you call me?   Call me!

5. REFLEXIVE PRONOUNS

The reflexive pronoun shows that the action is being performed both by and to the subject. Only certain verbs have reflexive forms. Most often reflexives will show up as incorrect answer choices.

Tu te laves.   *Tu te laves les mains.*
    You wash yourself.   You wash your hands.

me	myself	*nous*	ourselves
te	yourself	*vous*	yourselves or yourself (formal)
se	himself/herself	*se*	themselves

You might also see *moi-même, toi-même, lui-même/elle-même, soi-même* (oneself), *nous-mêmes, vous-même(s), eux-mêmes / elles-mêmes*. They would be used as stressed pronouns would be.

PRONOUN SUMMARY

The following are the pronouns you should know. **You're most likely to be tested on third person singular and plural,** since those are the forms that change the most.

Subjects	Objects		Reflexive	Stressed
	Direct	Indirect		
je	*me (m')*	*me (m')*	*me (m')*	*moi*
tu	*te (t')*	*te (t')*	*te (t')*	*toi*
il, elle	*le, la (l')*	*lui*	*se (s')*	*lui, elle, soi*
nous	*nous*	*nous*	*nous*	*nous*
vous	*vous*	*vous*	*vous*	*vous*
ils, elles	*les*	*leur*	*se (s')*	*eux, elles*

Because this is a multiple-choice test, you will be asked which of four pronouns go into the blank. Notice that some pronouns are always the same: *nous* and *vous*.

nous or vous can be: subject or
                                           direct object or
                                           indirect object or
                                           stressed or reflexive

lui can be: indirect object or
                                           stressed

Let's try it out.

Paul voulait _____ faire peur.

(A) elle
(B) la
(C) lui
(D) les

Does the missing pronoun here serve as a subject or object? It serves as an object, so we can eliminate (A). *Elle* serves only as a subject pronoun or a stressed pronoun. We won't use a stressed pronoun because a preposition is not being used.

Does the verb *faire peur* take a direct or indirect object? Indirect. In English, "to frighten someone" takes a direct object, but in French the expression is *faire peur* **à** *quelqu'un*.

Often, three choices will refer to one person, the fourth to more than one person. In most cases, the one that is different will be wrong.

Let's cross out (D) *les*, which is a direct object pronoun as well as the only plural pronoun.

So, which choice is an indirect object pronoun?

Lui, (C), is the indirect pronoun for third person singular. It is the right answer. *La*, (B), is the direct object pronoun.

Je suis allé au concert sans _____.

(A) leur
(B) tu
(C) le
(D) eux

What type of pronoun would come after *sans*? A stressed pronoun comes after a preposition. Which of the answer choices is a stressed pronoun? Only (D). *Eux* is the stressed pronoun meaning "them." (A) is an indirect object pronoun. (B) is a subject pronoun. (C) is a direct object pronoun. (D) is the correct answer: *Je suis allé au concert sans eux.*

MORE TYPES OF PRONOUNS

You also want to be familiar with some other types of pronouns that may show up. The following are most likely to be given in the real test as incorrect answer choices.

Possessive pronouns

Possessive pronouns agree in gender and number with the noun that they replace.

Ce livre est à Nathalie.
> This book is Nathalie's.

C'est le sien.
> It is hers.
> (use of possessive pronoun)

Cette montre est à Pierre.
> This watch is Pierre's.

C'est la sienne.
> It is his.

Singular pronouns

le mien / la mienne
le tien / la tienne
le sien / la sienne

le nôtre / la nôtre
le vôtre / la vôtre
le leur / la leur

Ce livre est à toi.
> This book is yours.

C'est le tien.
> It is yours.

Plural pronouns

les miens / les miennes
les tiens / les tiennes
les siens / les siennes

les nôtres
les vôtres
les leurs

Ces chaussures sont à elles.
> These shoes are theirs.

Ce sont les leurs.
> They are theirs.

Possessive pronouns must always be used with an article (*le, la, les*).

Person	Singular		Plural	
	Masc.	**Fem.**	**Masc.**	**Fem.**
je	*le mien*	*la mienne*	*les miens*	*les miennes*
tu	*le tien*	*la tienne*	*les tiens*	*les tiennes*
il, elle	*le sien*	*la sienne*	*les siens*	*les siennes*
nous	*le nôtre*	*la nôtre*	*les nôtres**	
vous	*le vôtre*	*la vôtre*	*les vôtres**	
ils, elles	*le leur*	*la leur*	*les leurs**	

* These represent both the masculine and the feminine forms.

STILL MORE TYPES OF PRONOUNS

About half of the pronoun questions revolve around the use of other types of pronouns (adverbial pronouns, demonstrative pronouns, relative pronouns, indefinite pronouns, etc.). Don't worry—you don't need to know the terminology.

Example:

Je n'ai pas le temps de faire les courses ------- ma mère m'a demandé de faire.

- (A) qui
- (B) que
- (C) dont
- (D) lesquelles

Which pronoun is correct?
Let's take a look at each in turn and see what rules govern their use.

Qui—who or which or that

Qui is the equivalent of the English "who," except that *qui* can also be used to refer to things ("that"). **The *qui* refers to the subject of the phrase**.

la dame qui danse là-bas...
> the lady who is dancing over there...

la table qui est cassée...
> the table that is broken...

Qui can also be used with a preposition. In this case, it can only refer to a person.

l'homme sans qui je n'aurais rien accompli...
> the man without whom I would have accomplished nothing...

Que—whom or that

Que is used in a number of ways in the French language. On the SAT French, however, it usually shows up as a relative pronoun. Roughly the equivalent of the English "whom," it **refers to** the person or thing that is **the object** of the action. *Que* is **never used with a preposition**.

l'enfant que j'ai puni...
(i.e., *j'ai puni l'enfant*)
> the child whom I punished...

la bicyclette que j'ai reçue pour mon anniversaire...
(i.e., *j'ai reçu la bicyclette pour mon anniversaire*)
> the bicycle that I received for my birthday...

Qui vs. Que

Don't use your ear to determine if *qui* or *que* is right. Learn a few rules that will help you choose: 1. Is the noun before the blank the subject or object of the phrase? 2. Is there a preposition involved?

When do you use *qui* and when do you use *que*?

Unless there is a preposition involved, this is similar to the English use of "who" or "whom." In English, one test is to see if the "who" or "whom" would be replaced by "he" or "him," and see which sounds right:

> *the man _____ is smoking over there. . .*
>> "He" is smoking, so you would use "who."

> *the man _____ I hugged. . .*
>> I hugged "him," so you would use "whom."

If you understand "who/whom" in English, you may want to translate and decide if "who" or "whom" is correct. If "who" is correct, use *qui*; if "whom" is correct, use *que*.

> *l'homme qui fume là-bas. . .*
>> the man who is smoking over there. . .

> *l'homme que j'ai embrassé. . .*
>> the man whom I hugged. . .

What if a preposition is involved?

If there is a preposition before the blank, you use *qui* if referring to a person and the correct form of *lequel* if referring to a thing or a person. You never use *que* immediately following a preposition.

If a preposition is involved and the pronoun **refers to a person,** use *qui* or the correct form of *lequel*.

> *l'homme **à qui** j'ai donné de l'argent…*
>> the man **to whom** I gave money…

> *l'ami **pour lequel** j'ai acheté un chapeau…*
>> the friend **for whom** I bought a hat…

> *la jeune fille **pour laquelle** j'ai fait une robe…*
>> the girl **for whom** I made a dress…

lequel, laquelle
lesquels, lesquelles

Lequel is used with a preposition if the pronoun **refers to people or things.** The form of *lequel* agrees in gender and number with the person(s) or thing(s) it refers to.

Note that if a preposition is involved and the pronoun **refers to a thing,** use **only *lequel*** (in its correct form).

> *l'argent **avec lequel** j'ai payé la facture…*
>> the money **with which** I paid the bill…

> *les cerises **pour lesquelles** j'ai payé trop cher…*
>> the cherries for which I paid too much…

Quoi—which or what

Quoi is used to **refer to things only**. It is usually used with a preposition when asking a question.

> *À quoi pensez-vous?*
>> What are you thinking of?

> *De quoi parlez-vous?*
>> What are you talking about?

Dont—of whom or of which

You can use *dont* only if the verb in the clause that it introduces takes *de* as a preposition. *Dont* can be used with both people and things.

> *l'amie dont j'ai tellement parlé (parler de)*. . .
>> the friend of whom I have spoken so much . . .

Technically, in the above example, you could also say, *l'amie de qui j'ai tellement parlé;* however, *dont* is preferred. On this test, you'll never have to choose between the two forms.

Notice that *dont* can never be used to begin a question.

> *La robe dont j'ai envie*. . .
>> but
> *De quelle robe avez-vous envie?*

Dont is a favorite answer choice of the writers of the SAT French. Why? Because it hangs on a little rule. For *dont* to be correct, it **must be used with a verb that normally takes *de*.**

Now let's go back to our example first given at the top of page 61.

> Je n'ai pas le temps de faire les courses _____ ma mère m'a demandé de faire.
>
> (A) qui
> (B) que
> (C) dont
> (D) lesquelles

Dont will be correct only if the verb in the phrase is one that takes *de* as a preposition.

Is a preposition involved? No. Get rid of (D) *lesquelles*. You can also get rid of (A) *qui*, because where objects are concerned, *qui* is used only with a preposition.

Does *faire* take *de* as a preposition? No. Eliminate (C) *dont*. The answer must be (B) *que*.

> Voilà l'ami _____ j'ai passé l'été.
>
> (A) chez qui
> (B) à qui
> (C) que
> (D) dont

Can *de* be used as a preposition following *passer l'été*? No. Eliminate (D).

Can *passer l'été* be used without a preposition? No. Eliminate (C) *que*.

Can *passer l'été* be used with *chez*? Yes. *Passer l'été chez* means "to spend the summer at the home of." (A) is the right answer.

You can use *à* with *passer l'été*, but in that case it would be used with a place, not with a person. Eliminate (B).

> *J'ai passé beaucoup de temps à la bibliothèque.*
>> I spent a lot of time at the library.

Voilà la bibliothèque où j'ai passé beaucoup de temps.

Here is the library where I spent a lot of time.

Où — where

Où and *dans lequel* sometimes mean the same thing. You'll never be asked to choose between the two.

J'ai vu l'hôpital où je suis né.

I saw the hospital where I was born.

In many cases, *où* can be replaced by *dans lequel*.

En — of it/of them

En replaces a noun that is used with a verb that takes the preposition *de*. It can be used for people or things. It is often used in sentences that refer to a number or quantity of things.

Nous parlons du livre.

We are speaking about the book.

Nous en parlons.

We are speaking about it.

Think of *en* as meaning "of it" or "of them." You can use it in some cases where the *de* is understood but not actually used.

J'ai des cassettes.

I have some tapes.

J'ai cinq cassettes.

I have five tapes.

J'en ai cinq.

I have five of them.

While *en* will usually refer to some kind of possession, it can also be used to indicate place or location if the verb in question uses *de*.

Il vient de Rome.

He comes from Rome.

Il en vient.

He's coming from there.

Y — there

Y often refers to place or location. *Y* replaces a phrase that begins with prepositions that indicate place (*à, chez, dans, sur*).

Est-ce que tu vas à la fête?

Are you going to the party?

Oui, j'y vais.

Yes, I am going there.

Y also replaces a phrase that begins with the preposition *à* and a thing.

Jouez-vous au tennis?
> Do you play tennis?

Oui, j'y joue.
> Yes, I do.

As-tu réfléchi à ta dissertation?
> Have you thought about your essay?

Oui, j'y ai réfléchi.
> Yes, I have.

Aucun — not one, none

Aucun, *aucune* is always used with *ne.*

Aucune de ces réponses n'est correcte.
> None of these answers is correct.

Avez-vous des stylos? -------.

- (A) Oui, lesquels.
- (B) Oui, j'ai quelques.
- (C) Non, je n'en ai aucun.
- (D) Non, je n'ai pas.

(A) *lesquels* cannot stand by itself in a sentence unless it is an answer to a question (*Apporte-moi les stylos. Lesquels?*). Eliminate it.

(B) *quelques,* meaning "some," is an adjective and can only be used to modify a noun (*j'ai quelques stylos* or *j'en ai quelques-uns*). Eliminate it.

(C) *aucun* is used with *ne.* This is correct.

(D) By itself, *je n'ai pas* does not work. It lacks a reference to what it is that I do not have. To be correct, you would need to say either *je n'en ai pas* or *je n'ai pas de stylos.*

Personne — no one

Like *aucun,* *personne* is used with *ne.*

Personne n'a téléphoné aujourd'hui.
> No one telephoned today.

Personne can be used without *ne* only if it is a one-word answer to a question.

Qui a cassé ce vase? Personne.
> Who broke this vase? No one.

Qui va chercher le paquet à la poste?————————vais.

- (A) Quoi
- (B) J'y
- (C) Personne
- (D) J'en

(A) *Quoi* does not work and makes no sense. It refers to things and is usually used with a preposition.

(B) is correct. The *y* replaces the expression *à la poste.*

> Both *aucun* and *personne* must be used with *ne* in a sentence.

(C) has two problems. First, *personne* needs to be used with *ne*. Second, *personne* takes the third person singular form of the verb (in this case, *va*).

(D) *En* is used to show either possession or to replace a noun that works with a verb that takes *de*. Here the verb is *aller* and it takes the preposition *à*. So *en* is not correct.

The following pronouns may or may not show up on the test:

Chacun — each one

> *Chacun à son goût.*
>> Each one to his own taste.
>> (The saying: to each his own)

Quelque chose — something

> *Je vous ai acheté quelque chose à la pâtisserie.*
>> I bought you something at the pastry shop.

Quelqu'un — someone

> *Quelqu'un a volé ma moto!*
>> Someone stole my motorbike!

PRONOUN QUESTIONS

1. ------- est arrivé à Paul hier?

    (A) Quel
    (B) Quoi
    (C) Qu'
    (D) Qu'est-ce qui

2. C'est -------.

    (A) eux
    (B) il
    (C) lui
    (D) le

3. C'est grâce à ------- que nous avons pu venir.

    (A) eux
    (B) les
    (C) leur
    (D) ils

4. La chose la plus difficile est de ------- réveiller le matin.

    (A) lui
    (B) il
    (C) le
    (D) moi

5. ------- a sorti la poubelle.

   (A) Il n'
   (B) Personne n'
   (C) Aucun
   (D) Qui

EXPLANATIONS OF PRONOUN QUESTIONS

1. ------- *est arrivé à Paul hier?*

   What happened to Paul yesterday?

(A) *Quel*

Quel means "which" and is used to modify a noun (*Quelle voiture est la vôtre?*). We need something that means "what."

(B) *Quoi*

In questions, *quoi* is used only with a preposition (*À quoi sert cet exercice?*).

(C) *Qu'*

Qu' is a shortened form of *que*. Since the "what" of the question is the subject (what happened), it cannot be *que*.

(D) *Qu'est-ce qui* is correct. You cannot use *qui* alone because that would mean "who happened to Paul yesterday?" And you need *qui* here because it is directly followed by a verb.

2. *C'est -------.*

   It is he.

With *c'est* or *ce sont* you use either a noun or a stressed pronoun.

(A) *eux*

Eux is a stressed pronoun, which is correct, but since it is plural, the correct sentence would be *ce sont eux*.

(B) *il*

Il is a subject pronoun. No good here.

(C) *lui*

Lui can be a singular stressed pronoun. This is the correct answer.

(D) *le*

Le is a direct object pronoun. Cancel it.

3. *C'est grâce à ------- que nous avons pu venir.*

   It is thanks to them that we could come.

Because the pronoun is being used with a preposition (but not as an indirect object), we want a stressed pronoun.

(A) *eux*

Eux is a stressed pronoun, so this is the correct choice.

(B) *les*

Les is the direct object pronoun.

(C) *leur*

Leur is the indirect object pronoun.

(D) *ils*

Ils is the subject pronoun.

4. *La chose la plus difficile est de ------- réveiller le matin.*

    The most difficult thing is to wake him up in the morning.

The verb in this sentence is *réveiller*, a verb that takes a direct object. The correct answer must serve as a direct object pronoun.

(A) *lui*

Lui can be an indirect object pronoun or a stressed pronoun.

(B) *il*

Il is the subject pronoun.

(C) *le*

Le is the direct object pronoun, so this is the correct answer.

(D) *moi*

Moi is the stressed pronoun.

5. *------- a sorti la poubelle.*

    No one took out the garbage.

(A) *Il n'*

This choice does not work because the sentence lacks the *pas* that must be used with *ne* (*n'*) to make a negative.

(B) *Personne n'*

This is the correct answer. *Personne* **must be used with** *ne* **and does not need the** *pas*.

(C) *Aucun*

Like *personne*, *aucun* must be used with *ne* unless it is the one-word answer to a question.

(D) *Qui*

Qui can begin the sentence in a question, but not in a statement.

VERBS

There are three types of verb questions: use of the subjunctive, agreement of the past participle, and tense.

KNOW THE SUBJUNCTIVE

About 25 percent of the grammar questions on the test deal with verb use. Over half of them ask you to decide whether or not to use the subjunctive.

What is the subjunctive?

Like the indicative, the subjunctive is not a tense; it is a mode or mood. While it is not often used in English, it is used very frequently in French. This is why it is always found in the SAT French Subject Test.

When do you use the subjunctive?

In French and on the SAT French, you will use the subjunctive in phrases that follow expressions of doubt, suggestion, preference, desire, improbability, or emotion. The subjunctive is also used with certain conjunctions. All phrases that require use of the subjunctive will contain the word *que*.

EXPRESSIONS THAT TAKE THE SUBJUNCTIVE

Doubt or Uncertainty

Je doute qu'il réussisse son examen.
　　I doubt that he will pass his exam.

J'ai peur qu'il rate son examen.
　　I am afraid that he will fail his exam.

Je ne crois pas que vous ayez raison.
　　I don't believe that you are right.

Il est douteux qu'elle vienne ce weekend.
　　It's doubtful that she will come this weekend.

Il est possible que j'aie tort.
　　I may be wrong (It is possible that I am wrong).

Suggestion or Preference

Je préfère que vous rentriez tout de suite.
　　I prefer that you return at once.

J'insiste pour que tu sois à l'heure.
　　I insist that you be on time.

Il vaut mieux que vous ne sortiez pas ce soir.
　　It is better that you do not go out tonight.

Il est important que vous étudiiez l'emploi du subjonctif.
　　It is important that you study the use of the subjunctive.

Il faut que je prenne un rendez-vous chez le dentiste.
　　It is necessary that I make an appointment at the dentist's.

> All phrases that require use of the subjunctive will contain the word *que*.

Desire

Je veux que tu travailles plus sérieusement.
　　I want you to work more seriously.

Je souhaite que tout se passe bien.
　　I wish that everything goes well.

Je désire qu'il soit heureux.
　　I want him to be happy.

Improbability

Il est peu probable qu'il neige demain.
    It is unlikely that it will snow tomorrow.

Note: **Do not use the subjunctive with probability:**
Il est probable qu'il pleuvra demain.
    It is likely that it will rain tomorrow.

Emotion

Je suis étonné qu'il ne soit pas encore là.
    I am surprised that he is not yet here.

Je suis content que tout se soit bien passé.
    I am happy that everything went well.

Je regrette que le temps passe si vite.
    I am sorry that time goes by so quickly.

CONJUNCTIONS THAT TAKE THE SUBJUNCTIVE

pour que
    so that

quoique, bien que
    although

> The subjunctive is used
> with expressions of doubt,
> preference, or emotion.

pourvu que
    so long as, provided that

à moins que
    unless

jusqu'à ce que
    until

avant que (but not *après que*)
    before

The subjunctive is also used to express an opinion with superlatives.

C'est le film le plus stupide que j'aie jamais vu.
    It is the stupidest movie I have ever seen.

The French assume that you cannot know for a fact if something is absolutely the worst or the best if the statement is based on personal experience.

So now what?

You won't have to construct the subjunctive of a given verb; you only need to recognize it among the four answer choices. In addition to the present subjunctive, you may also see the past of the subjunctive. You'll recognize it because the auxiliary or helper verb (*avoir* or *être*) will be in the subjunctive. Note that with *avoir*, *il a* becomes *il ait* and with *être*, *il est* becomes *il soit*.

PRESENT TENSE

Certain: *Je sais qu'il vient ce soir.*
            I know that he is coming tonight.

Uncertain: *Je doute qu'il vienne ce soir.*
(Pres. Subj.)   I doubt that he is coming tonight.

PAST TENSE

Certain: *Je sais qu'il est venu hier.*
            I know that he came yesterday.

Uncertain: *Je doute qu'il soit venu hier.*
(Past Subj.)   I doubt that he came yesterday.

Now you try it:

Jean-Paul ne m'a pas téléphoné; j'ai peur qu'il ------- oublié notre rendez-vous.

(A) a
(B) avait
(C) ait
(D) aura

Does the expression *J'ai peur que* . . . take the subjunctive? Yes! It shows doubt, fear, or uncertainty. The answer is (C).
    Try another one:

Ma mère m'a grondée quand elle ------- ma robe déchirée.

(A) voit
(B) a vu
(C) voie
(D) ait vu

Does the expression *Ma mère m'a grondée quand* . . . take the subjunctive?
No. The verb in this case (*voir*) is an actual event. Eliminate (C) and (D). This sentence requires the past, so the answer is (B). Also, note that we have *quand* here and not *que*.

Détruisez les preuves avant qu'il ------- ce que nous avons fait.

(A) apprendra
(B) apprenne
(C) apprendrait
(D) apprend

Is *avant que* a conjunction that takes the subjunctive?
Yes. The answer is (B). (A) is the future. (C) is the conditional. (D) is the present.

TENSE

You remember all those fancy verb tenses you learned in French class: the *passé simple*, the future perfect, the pluperfect subjunctive? Well, for the purposes of this test, you can forget them.

For the SAT French, you need to recognize the present, the imperfect, the *passé composé*, the future, the conditional, the past of the conditional, and the *plus-que-parfait*, and you must know when to use them. The subjunctive, actually a mode or mood rather than a tense, is the verb form most frequently tested. The conditional, also a mode or mood, is the next most frequently tested verb form.

Le présent

This is pretty straightforward. It's the form of the verb you're most used to seeing.

> *Il part.*

L'imparfait

The imperfect tense is a form of the past that indicates something was ongoing: either something that went on for a period of time in the past or something that happened repeatedly in the past.

présent	*imparfait*
Il part.	*Il partait.*

Le passé composé

This tense indicates that a past action (or state) is now complete. It is made up of an auxiliary verb (either *avoir* or *être* in the present tense) and a past participle. It indicates something that started and ended in the past and is now over.

présent	*passé composé*
Il part.	*Il est parti.*

Le plus-que-parfait (past imperfect)

The past imperfect indicates that something happened in the past prior to another action in the past. It is made up of an auxiliary verb (*avoir* or *être* in the imperfect tense) and a past participle.

présent	*plus-que-parfait*
Il part.	*Il était parti.*

The *Passé Composé* vs. the *Imparfait*

Notice the difference between the *passé composé* and the imperfect. The *passé composé* describes a one-time action that is now complete, while the imperfect describes an action that was ongoing in the past.

Le futur

This indicates that something will happen in the future.

présent	*futur*
Il part.	*Il partira.*

Le conditionnel

The conditional mode or mood indicates something that would happen if a set of requirements were met.

présent	*conditionnel*
Il part.	*Il partirait.*

Use of the conditional

Almost half of the questions that relate to verb sequence tests you on the use of the conditional. The conditional is used in a sentence that follows a clause that begins with *si* and uses the imperfect tense.

> *Si + imparfait → conditionnel*

> *Si j'avais le temps, je le ferais moi-même.*
> > If I had the time, I would do it myself.

If the past imperfect is used, then the past conditional will be used.

> *si + plus-que-parfait → conditionnel passé*

> *Si j'avais eu le temps, je l'aurais fait moi-même.*
> > If I had had the time, I would have done it myself.

Présent	*Aujourd'hui, il fait ses devoirs.*
Passé composé	*Hier il a fait ses devoirs.*
Imparfait	*Quand il était petit, il faisait ses devoirs.*
Futur	*Demain, il fera ses devoirs.*
Conditionnel	*S'il avait des devoirs, il les ferait.*

The conditional is actually a mode or mood, not a tense. It is used to describe if/then situations.

You will use the conditional before or after clauses that start with *si* and contain the imperfect.

Sequence of tenses

In any question with several verbs, the tenses must follow in a logical sequence.

S'il avait des devoirs, il les **ferait.**
S'il **avait eu** des devoirs, il les **aurait faits.**

Si j'étais riche, je ------- un yacht.

(A) m'achète
(B) m'achèterai
(C) m'achetais
(D) m'achèterais

What tense is correct here? Because *si* is used with the imperfect, the following verb must be the conditional.

How do we recognize the conditional? It combines the structure of the future with the endings of the imperfect (*ais*, *ait*, etc.). (D) is the correct choice.

Avant d'entrer au restaurant, il m'a demandé si j'
------- assez d'argent pour payer le dîner.

(A) ai
(B) avais
(C) ai eu
(D) aurai

What tense is correct here? (A) cannot be correct. It is the present tense, and the previous clause, *il m'a demandé*, tells us the action is in the past. Since (D) is the future, we can eliminate it as well.

Do we use the imperfect or the past? (C) implies that having enough money was an event or action that occurred once prior to the question. Because we have the phrase, *avant d'entrer*, we know that the state of having money is an ongoing one, preceding and presumably continuing throughout dinner. (B) is the correct answer.

Make sure you can identify which tense (or mode) is which.

It is important that you recognize what each tense or mood looks like when you see it. Usually the ending of the verb will give you a clue.

Présent	Imparfait	Passé composé	Plus-que-parfait
je donne	je donnais	j'ai donné	j'avais donné
tu donnes	tu donnais	tu as donné	tu avais donné
il donne	il donnait	il a donné	il avait donné
nous donnons	nous donnions	nous avons donné	nous avions donné
vous donnez	vous donniez	vous avez donné	vous aviez donné
ils donnent	ils donnaient	ils ont donné	ils avaient donné

Futur	Conditionnel	Subjonctif présent	Conditionnel passé
je donnerai	je donnerais	que je donne	j'aurais donné
tu donneras	tu donnerais	que tu donnes	tu aurais donné
il donnera	il donnerait	qu'il donne	il aurait donné
nous donnerons	nous donnerions	que nous donnions	nous aurions donné
vous donnerez	vous donneriez	que vous donniez	vous auriez donné
elles donneront	ils donneraient	qu'ils donnent	elles auraient donné

With *donner*, as in all regular "*er*" verbs, the singular forms of the subjunctive present are identical to the indicative present.

AVOIR VS. ÊTRE

PAST PARTICIPLE AGREEMENT

What is a past participle?

A past participle is the form of the verb that combines with "to have" (in English), or *être* or *avoir* (in French), in order to make the past tense.

Je mange mon petit déjeuner.
    I eat my breakfast (present).

*J'ai **mangé** mon petit déjeuner.*
    I have **eaten** my breakfast (past).

You'll most likely be given the choice of four different forms of the past participle—masculine singular, feminine singular, masculine plural, and feminine plural—with an occasional infinitive thrown in to confuse you. You must decide which is correct.

When does the past participle agree, and with what?

The past participle **agrees with the subject** of the sentence **when**:

> The verb takes *être* as its auxiliary verb:

*Pauline et Chantal sont par**ties** hier pour l'Afrique.*
    Pauline and Chantal left yesterday for Africa.

> The verb is **reflexive**, and therefore takes *être*:

*Elle s'est évanou**ie** quand elle a entendu la nouvelle.*
    She fainted when she heard the news.

> The past participle will agree with the <u>subject</u> if the verb takes *être* or is reflexive.
> It will agree with the <u>object</u> of the sentence if the verb takes *avoir* and the direct object is before the verb.

The past participle **agrees with the direct object** of the sentence **when**:

> The verb takes *avoir* and the **direct object** is placed **before the verb** (often in the form of a pronoun):

*J'ai aidé mes **amies**.*
    (no agreement)
    I helped my friends.

*Je **les** ai aid**ées**.*
    (agreement)
    I helped them.

Since questions in Part C often contain several sentences, information about the gender and number may come earlier than the sentence in which the blank appears. Try this:

> Les deux soeurs ont très bien ———— à l'université.
>
> (A) réussi
> (B) réussie
> (C) réussis
> (D) réussies

The verb *réussir* (to succeed, to be successful) uses the auxiliary verb *avoir*. Is there a direct object that precedes the verb? No. There is no direct object in this sentence. The correct answer is (A).

> La fille à côté de moi m'a donné les renseignements
> dont j'avais besoin. Je l'ai -------.
>
> (A) remercié
> (B) remerciée
> (C) remerciées
> (D) remercier

The verb *remercier* (to thank) also takes *avoir* as its helper verb. Is there a direct object before the verb? Yes, "*l'*" refers to *la fille*. The correct answer is (B).

ODDBALL VERB FORMS: OTHER PARTICIPLES

There is a small chance that you will have a question or two on other participles: the present participle, the gerund, or the perfect participle. You don't need to know these terms, just recognize how they work in a sentence. This type of question is most likely to appear on Part C, where you choose the appropriate form of the verb based on the sequence of tenses in the paragraph.

The present participle

The present participle is a verb form that ends in "-ing" in English. It shows that one action is happening at the same time as another.

> *J'ai vu les enfants courant sur la pelouse.*
> I saw the children running on the lawn.

The present participle "running" is also acting as an adjective, describing something about the children.

The gerund

The gerund is also like an "-ing" verb form in English, but in this case, it is acting as an adverb rather than an adjective. In French, it is always accompanied by the preposition *en*. It can show:

- **That one action is happening at the same time as another**

   Elle montait l'escalier en chantant.
   She climbed the stairs while singing.

- **That one action is part of a process**

   En lisant, nous découvrons de nouveaux mondes.
   In reading, we discover new worlds.

The perfect participle

The perfect participle (made up of *ayant* or *étant* + the past participle) is the past tense of the present participle. An example in English would be "having won the war, the army celebrated." This form is used to show that one action was completed before another began.

> ***Ayant fini*** *le repas, nous avons débarrassé la table.*
> Having finished the meal, we cleared the table.

If the verb takes *être*, you will see *étant* instead of *ayant*:

> ***Étant montée***, *elle ne pouvait plus entendre la discussion.*
> Having gone upstairs, she could no longer hear the discussion.

VERB QUESTIONS

1. Si -------, je préparerais le dîner.

   (A) vous en avez envie
   (B) on me le demande
   (C) j'avais le temps
   (D) tu seras d'accord

2. Paul regrette que nous ------- pas réussi.

   (A) n'avons
   (B) n'avions
   (C) n'ayons
   (D) n'aurons

3. ------- une lettre quand on a sonné à la porte.

   (A) J'écris
   (B) J'écrirais
   (C) J'écrive
   (D) J'écrivais

4. Elle n'a jamais oublié ce que nous ------- au moment de son départ.

   (A) disons
   (B) ayons dit
   (C) avons dit
   (D) aurions dit

5. Est-ce que vous ------- contents si je n'avais pas accepté l'invitation?

   (A) êtes
   (B) soyez
   (C) étiez
   (D) auriez été

6. Nous doutons ------- leur rendre visite chez eux.

   (A) qu'il ait le temps de
   (B) qu'il voudrait
   (C) qu'il peut
   (D) qu'elle avait envie de

7. -------, elle est partie pour le long trajet chez elle.

   (A) Disait au revoir
   (B) Dire au revoir
   (C) Ayant dit au revoir
   (D) Avoir dit au revoir

EXPLANATIONS OF VERB QUESTIONS

1. *Si -------, je préparerais le dîner.*

   If I had time, I would make dinner.

Since the conditional tense is used in the portion of the sentence following the blank, the verb that precedes it must be in the **imperfect**. Only choice (C) has a verb in the imperfect.

   (A) *vous en avez envie*—present

   (B) *on me le demande*—present

   (C) *j'avais le temps*—imperfect

   (D) *tu seras d'accord*—future

2. *Paul regrette que nous ------- pas réussi.*

   Paul regrets that we have not succeeded.

What mode is used with verbs like *regretter que*? The subjunctive. Only choice (C) has the subjunctive.

   (A) *n'avons*—present

   (B) *n'avions*—imperfect

   (C) *n'ayons*—subjunctive (present)

   (D) *n'aurons*—future

3. *------- une lettre quand on a sonné à la porte.*

   I was writing a letter when the doorbell rang.

The use of the *passé composé* indicates that the sentence takes place in the past, so you can eliminate (A), (B), and (C). The answer is (D). The use of the imperfect indicates that the action of letter writing was ongoing when the doorbell rang.

(A) *J'écris*—present

(B) *J'écrirais*—conditional

(C) *J'écrive*—subjunctive (present)

(D) *J'écrivais*—imperfect

4. *Elle n'a jamais oublié ce que nous ------- au moment de son départ.*

She never forgot what we said at the moment of her departure

Does the expression *ce que* take the subjunctive? No. Eliminate (B). The use of the *passé composé* in the first part of the sentence indicates that the sentence takes place in the past. Eliminate (A) and (D). The correct answer is (C).

(A) *disons*—present

(B) *ayons dit*—past of the subjunctive

(C) *avons dit*—*passé composé*

(D) *aurions dit*—past of the conditional

5. *Est-ce que vous ------- contents si je n'avais pas accepté l'invitation?*

Would you have been happy if I had not accepted the invitation?

Since a form of the imperfect is being used with *si*, the other verb must be in the conditional. (D) is the only verb in the conditional. Since one part of the sentence has the past form of the imperfect (*the plus-que-parfait*), it makes sense that the conditional verb would also be in a past form.

(A) *êtes*—present

(B) *soyez*—subjunctive

(C) *étiez*—imperfect

(D) *auriez été*—past of the conditional

6. *Nous doutons ------- leur rendre visite chez eux.*

We doubt that he has time to visit them.

Does the verb *douter que* take the subjunctive? Yes, so (B), (C), and (D) must be wrong. (A) is the correct answer because the subjunctive is used.

(A) *qu'il ait le temps de*—subjunctive

(B) *qu'il voudrait*—conditional

(C) *qu'il peut*—present

(D) *qu'elle avait envie de*—imperfect

7. ------- , *elle est partie pour le long trajet chez elle.*

> Having said goodbye, she left for the long journey home.

We need a verb form that shows when she said goodbye (the verb is in all the answer choices). We can eliminate (B), since it is the infinitive and the sentence is in the past. To show that she said goodbye either before or as she left, we need either the perfect or the present participle. The only participle here is (C), the perfect participle, "having said goodbye." This is our answer. The other choices, (A) and (D), cannot be used by themselves in a phrase.

(A) *Disait au revoir*—imperfect

(B) *Dire au revoir*—infinitive

(C) ***Ayant dit au revoir*—perfect participle**

(D) *Avoir dit au revoir*—past infinitive

PREPOSITIONS

Below is a list of the most important prepositions for you to know.

Common Prepositions	
à	= to
de	= from, of
sur	= on
sous	= under
pour	= for
avant (+ nom)	= before
avant de (+ verbe)	= before
après	= after
chez	= at, to (location)
en	= of, in, from, to
dans	= in, into
entre	= between
pendant	= during
vers	= toward
sans	= without
sauf	= except, unless
selon	= according to
durant	= during
malgré, en dépit de	= in spite of
afin de	= in order to

Prepositions are tested on Part A (one or two questions) and on Part B. Prepositions join words and have specific meanings. Prepositions are also a part of grammar, as certain verbs can only be used with certain prepositions.

Just as in English, certain verbs or expressions in French require prepositions while others require none. Memorization is the key here.

These questions will ask you for the preposition required. Some verbs can take more than one preposition depending on the meaning. In some questions, you will have the option of no preposition, denoted by a dash in the answer choice (——).

Il a refusé ------- faire son lit.

(A) ——
(B) à
(C) de
(D) sur

Out of context, *refuser* could take the preposition *à* or *de*, or no prepostion at all. Each has a different meaning.

refuser quelque chose—refuse something

> *Il a refusé l'offre.*
>> He refused the offer.

refuser quelque chose à quelqu'un—to deny something to someone

> *Le juge a refusé les droits de visite à la mère.*
>> The judge denied visitation rights to the mother.

refuser de faire quelque chose—to refuse to do something

> *L'enfant a refusé de manger ses carottes.*
>> The child refused to eat her carrots.

Which is appropriate for this question? Because someone is refusing to do something in this sentence, the correct answer is *de*, choice (C).

BACK TO PRONOUNS

Keep in mind that the verb's appropriate preposition may determine your choice of pronoun. If a verb requires a preposition in a given circumstance, for example, then you know that it takes an indirect and not a direct object. Or, if a given verb requires *de*, the relative pronoun used with it will reflect that.

> C'est la robe ------- j'ai envie.
>
> (A) que
> (B) qui
> (C) dont
> (D) à qui

The verb *avoir envie* takes the preposition *de*. (A) can be eliminated because *que* is never used with a preposition. (B) can also be eliminated because *qui* cannot be a subject here (*j'* is the subject). *Avoir envie* takes *de*, so (D), which is used with *à*, cannot be right. (C) *dont* is correct because *dont* in a sense means *de* + *que*.

Your knowledge of prepositions will affect your choice of pronouns. For example, *dont* will only be a correct choice if the verb takes *de* as a preposition.

Your experience studying French will probably provide you with a good sense of which verb takes which preposition, if you take the time to think about it. To refresh your memory, here is a partial list of verbs. Some never take a preposition, others sometimes take a preposition, and still others always take a preposition.

VERBS THAT DON'T TAKE A PREPOSITION

Verbs that don't take prepositions will be used with either the infinitive (the "to" form of a verb) or a direct object. Some verbs can be used with both.

pouvoir + infinitive	*Je peux faire n'importe quoi.* I can do anything I want.
espérer + infinitive	*J'espère venir demain.* I hope to come tomorrow.
vouloir + infinitive	*Je veux chanter.* I want to sing.
vouloir + object	*Je veux cette chemise.* I want this shirt.
mettre + object	*Il a mis le vase sur la table.* He put the vase on the table.
faire + object	*Marie a fait la vaisselle.* Marie washed the dishes.
acheter + object	*Il a acheté trois pantalons.* He bought three pairs of pants.

VERBS THAT SOMETIMES TAKE PREPOSITIONS AND SOMETIMES DON'T

aller + infinitive	*Je vais chercher ma soeur à l'école.* I am going to get my sister at school.
aller à	*Je vais aux États-Unis.* I am going to the United States.
refuser + object	*Je refuse l'offre.* I refuse the offer.
refuser de	*Je refuse de faire mes devoirs.* I refuse to do my homework.
oublier + object	*J'ai oublié mon stylo.* I forgot my pen.

A good resource to have on hand is a verb book. A good verb book will tell you how to conjugate a given verb and which prepositions are used with that verb.

oublier de	*J'ai oublié de dire au revoir.* I forgot to say good-bye.
accepter + **object**	*J'accepte votre invitation.* I accept your invitation.
accepter de	*J'accepte de nettoyer la cuisine.* I agree to clean the kitchen.
compter + **object**	*Je compte ma monnaie.* I am counting my change.
compter sur	*Nous comptons sur vous pour nous aider.* We count on you to help us.

VERBS THAT ALWAYS TAKE PREPOSITIONS

réfléchir à	*Je réfléchis à mon avenir.* I am thinking of my future.
penser à	*Je pense à ma mère.* I am thinking of my mother.

penser de	*Que pensez-vous du nouveau président?*
	    What do you think of (about) the
	    new president?

venir de	*Je viens d'Italie.* I come from Italy.

	Je viens de finir le chapitre.
	    I just finished the chapter.
	    I have just finished the chapter.

avoir envie de	*J'ai envie de manger.* I want to eat.
avoir besoin de	*J'ai besoin d'un crayon pour écrire.* I need a pencil to write.

There aren't any clear rules about when to use which preposition (aside from meaning). This is one place where you'll have to use your memory.

Set Expressions
Certain rules govern the use of some prepositions.

When discussing going to a country:

Je passe mes vacances . . .

Use *en* for feminine, singular countries.

en France
en Italie

Use *au* (*à* + *le*) for masculine, singular countries.

au Canada
au Brésil

Use *aux* (*à* + *les*) for plural countries, whether feminine or masculine.

aux États-Unis
aux Bermudes

When discussing being in or going to a town or city:

Je reste . . .
Je vais . . .

Use *à*:

à Paris
à New York
à Londres

> You always use the preposition *à* when referring to being in or going to a city.

When discussing coming from a country or town:

Il est venu . . .

Use *de* or *des* for feminine countries.

de Russie
d'Allemagne
des Bermudes

Use *du* or *des* for masculine countries.

du Japon
des Etats-Unis

Use *de* for all towns.
de Paris
de Lyon

List of Some Countries with Their Genders

Feminine	Masculine	Plural
la Russie	le Canada	les Etats-Unis (masc.)
la France	le Japon	les Pays-Bas (masc.)
l'Italie	le Brésil	les Bermudes (fem.)
l'Autriche	le Maroc	les Bahamas (fem.)
l'Allemagne	le Pérou	les Philippines (fem.)
la Belgique	le Vietnam	
la Grèce		
la Roumanie		
l'Espagne		

To tell what something is made of

Use *en*:

Il m'a donné un sac en cuir.
He gave me a leather bag.

Elle a fait une sculpture en verre.
She made a glass sculpture.

PREPOSITION QUESTIONS

1. Marie ------- les résultats de ses examens.

   (A) pense
   (B) attend
   (C) compte
   (D) a envie

2. Je ------- de leur écrire.

   (A) suis obligé
   (B) espère
   (C) veux
   (D) réfléchis

3. Je n'ai jamais eu l'occasion ------- voir ce film.

   (A) ——
   (B) à
   (C) de
   (D) sur

4. ------- le concert, elles bavardaient sans cesse.

   (A) Pendant
   (B) Dans
   (C) Avec
   (D) En

5. Je la vois souvent à -------.

   (A) France
   (B) ville
   (C) la boulangerie
   (D) loin

6. Elle n'a pas réfléchi ------- de refuser l'offre.

   (A) ——
   (B) avant
   (C) après
   (D) à

EXPLANATIONS OF PREPOSITION QUESTIONS

1. *Marie ------- les résultats de ses examens.*

    Marie is waiting for the results of her exams.

(A) *pense*
Penser requires the preposition *à* or *de*.
(B) *attend*
***Attendre* requires no preposition. This is the correct answer.**
(C) *compte*
Compter requires the preposition *sur*. Without a preposition, it means "to count" and makes no sense here.
(D) *a envie*
Avoir envie requires the preposition *de*.

2. *Je ------- de leur écrire.*

    I am obliged to write them.

(A) *suis obligé*
This is the correct answer. *Être obligé* requires the preposition *de*.
(B) *espère*
Espérer takes no preposition in French.
(C) *veux*
Vouloir takes no preposition. It cannot be used with *de*.
(D) *réfléchis*
Réfléchir takes the preposition *à*. It cannot be used with *de*.

3. *Je n'ai jamais eu l'occasion ------- voir ce film.*

   I have never had the opportunity to see this film.

The expression *avoir l'occasion* takes the preposition *de*. **(C) is the correct answer.**

4. *------- le concert, elles bavardaient sans cesse.*

   During the concert, they chattered endlessly.

(A) Pendant
Pendant means "during." This is the correct answer.
(B) *Dans*
Dans means "in." You cannot say *dans le concert*.
(C) *Avec*
Avec means "with." You might find a context in which *avec* works with *le concert*, but in this context, it does not.
(D) *En*
There might be a context where *en concert* is acceptable, but *en le concert* is never correct.

5. *Je la vois souvent à -------.*

   I see her often at the bakery.

(A) *France*
The correct expression would be *en France*.
(B) *ville*
You can say either *à la ville* or *en ville*.
(C) la boulangerie
This is the correct answer. You can say *à la boulangerie*.
(D) *loin*
Loin is never used with *à*.

6. *Elle n'a pas réfléchi ------- de refuser l'offre.*

   She did not think before refusing the offer.

(A) ——
Réfléchir must be used with a preposition.
(B) avant
This is the correct answer.
(C) *après*
You cannot say *après de. Après* is used with the infinitive (e.g., *après avoir réfléchi*).
(D) *à*
You cannot have these two prepositions, *à* and *de*, following each other.

ODDS AND ENDS

These topics will come up once or twice at most on the test.

ADJECTIVE VERSUS ADVERB

Adjectives modify nouns. Adverbs modify verbs, adjectives, and other adverbs. In French, adverbs often end in -*ment*.

> Elle a replacé le vase -------.
>
> (A) doux
> (B) brusquement
> (C) difficile
> (D) ennuyeuse

(A), (C), and (D) are all adjectives. (B) is the right answer.

When modifying an adjective, use the adverbs *trop, plus, très, si,* or *moins*. *Mieux*, like *pire*, cannot be used to modify an adjective.

> Ce cassoulet est ------- bon.
>
> (A) mieux
> (B) sans
> (C) si
> (D) pas

Bon is an adjective. The word in the blank must be an adverb. Only *si* is an adverb that can be used to modify an adjective. (C) is the right answer.

AVOIR VS. ÊTRE

When forming the *passé composé*, some verbs take *avoir* and some take *être*. To make a sweeping generalization, **most verbs take *avoir***, but verbs that indicate a **change of place** (*aller, venir, partir*) or **state** (*naître, mourir*) and **reflexive verbs** (*se laver, se coiffer*) **take *être***.

Verbs that Take *Être*					
monter	to go up	*rentrer*	to come back, to come/get in	*arriver*	to arrive
rester	to stay	*aller*	to go	*retourner*	to return
partir	to leave	*tomber*	to fall	*entrer*	to come in
venir	to come	*sortir*	to go out	*revenir*	to come back
descendre	to go down	*parvenir*	to succeed	*devenir*	to become
naître	to be born	*intervenir*	to intervene	*mourir*	to die
survenir	to happen	*passer*	to pass		

Odds and ends are just that: small, picky questions that show up from time to time but don't appear on every test.

Active vs. Passive

If you use *être* with the past participle of a verb that normally takes *avoir*, you are forming the passive tense of the verb.

Active (present)	Passive (present)
Le facteur distribue le courrier.	*Le courrier est distribué par le facteur.*
The postman delivers the mail.	The mail is delivered by the postman.

Possessive Adjectives

Possessive adjectives (not pronouns) show that a given noun belongs to a given person. But, unlike in English, French possessive adjectives agree with the gender and number of what is owned, not who owns it. The form of the adjective also changes depending on whether the noun begins with a vowel (or a silent "h").

Son is the masculine singular and *sa* is the feminine singular. **However, if a feminine noun begins with a vowel or a silent "h," the possessive adjective that goes with it will be *son*. *Sa* does not shorten to *s'*.**

> Elle avait de la soupe dans ------- assiette.
>
> (A) son
> (B) sa
> (C) s'
> (D) ses

Is *assiette* masculine or feminine? Singular or plural?

Assiette is feminine, but the word begins with a vowel; you can't say *sa assiette*, so eliminate (B). Possessive adjectives don't contract, so eliminate (C). *Assiette* is singular; cancel (D), which is plural. (A) is the right answer.

In French, you can't have a possessive adjective ending in a vowel sound (*ma, ta, sa*) in front of a word beginning with a vowel. You also can't shorten possessive adjectives the way you do pronouns. That is, even though *amie* is feminine, you <u>can't</u> say *sa amie* or *s'amie*. When you have a feminine noun that begins with a vowel, it will generally take the masculine version of the possessive adjective—in this case, *son amie*. The College Board loves to ask this kind of question.

	Only one object		More than one object
	masculin	*féminin*	*masculin et féminin*
One owner	mon livre	ma cravate	mes soeurs
	ton frère	ta santé	tes vacances
	son amie	sa voiture	ses cheveux
	masculin et féminin		*masculin et féminin*
More than one owner	notre professeur		nos voeux
	votre chemise		vos souhaits

SPECIAL POINTS FOR PART C

1. Is It Vocabulary or Grammar?

How can you tell? **A vocabulary question** will have **four words with clearly different meanings**. **A grammar question** will usually have **one word in four different forms** (for example, the same verb in four different tenses or with four different prepositions). When you see practice examples, the difference will be obvious.

2. Think of the Paragraph as a Whole

The paragraph is telling a story, so all sentences are connected. The key to this section is realizing that the correct answer can be based on both the sentence with the blank and on the sentences that precede it. **Don't think of each sentence as a separate question.**

3. Special Grammar Points

Some grammatical points are tested more frequently in Part C than in Part B. All the following points are thoroughly discussed earlier in this chapter.

Verb sequence

The action described in the paragraph must unfold **in a logical sequence. Make sure all the verbs** that you choose as answers **match the tense of the story.** Pay special attention to the rules for use of the imperfect and the conditional.

Agreement of the past participle

As we discussed earlier in this chapter, a past participle will agree with the *subject* if the verb takes *être*; if the verb takes *avoir* and the direct object comes before the verb, it will agree with the *object* of the sentence. In some cases, whether the direct object is masculine or feminine is revealed in a previous sentence.

> There are two kinds of pronoun questions on the test: one asks you to choose among the four main kinds of pronouns (subject, direct object, reflexive, indirect object, and stressed), and the other asks you to choose among pronouns like *qui, que, dont,* and *lequel.*

SUMMARY

These are the main points that the two grammatical sections (Parts B and C) will test.

I. Pronouns

A. subject/direct object/indirect object/stressed/reflexive pronouns

1. use stressed pronouns
   a. following a preposition
   b. as part of a compound subject or object
   c. as the object of the phrase *c'est* or *ce sont*
   d. as the one-word answer to a question

2. know which pronoun is in which form

B. choose among relative, indefinite, and other pronouns

1. *que*— with object
2. *qui* — with subject after a preposition when referring to people
3. *lequel* — after a preposition when referring to things or people
4. *dont*—when the verb in the clause normally takes *de*
5. *où* — to indicate place
6. *en* — to replace a noun used with *de*
7. *aucun* — not one or no one
8. *personne* — nobody
9. *y* — to indicate a place or a thing

II. VERBS

A.   use the subjunctive . . .

1. in expressions of doubt, fear, uncertainty, emotion
2. with certain conjunctions

B.   sequence of tenses

1. conditional is used after a clause that uses *si* with the imperfect

C.   agreement of past participle

1. with the subject with a verb that takes *être*
2. with the direct object placed before the verb that takes *avoir*

III. PREPOSITIONS

A.   use of prepositions

1. identify verb
2. identify meaning

B.   use of verb that fits preposition

1. determine what preposition the original verb requires
2. decide which answer choice uses the same preposition

IV. ODDS AND ENDS

A.   *avoir* vs. *être*
B.   active vs. passive
C.   adjective vs. adverb
D.   possessive adjectives

> Two verb forms which are heavily tested on the SAT French are the subjunctive and the conditional.

PRACTICE SECTION

Part B

<u>Directions:</u> Each of the following sentences contains a blank. From the four choices given, select the one that can be inserted in the blank to form a grammatically correct sentence. Choice (A) may consist of dashes that indicate that no insertion is required to form a grammatically correct sentence.

Answers can be found on pages 98–100.

1. Marie a ------- à m'offrir.

   (A) quelque chose
   (B) rien
   (C) plusieurs
   (D) quelque

2. Claude ------- de faire les courses.

   (A) a rejeté
   (B) a aimé
   (C) est obligé
   (D) a voulu

3. C'est grâce à son ------- qu'il a réussi.

   (A) talents
   (B) amie
   (C) gentillesse
   (D) oncles

4. Je ferai la vaisselle -------.

   (A) avant de partir
   (B) à tout à l'heure
   (C) hier
   (D) jamais

5. C'est ------- qui a gagné!

   (A) personne
   (B) je
   (C) leur
   (D) elle

6. Nos voisins ------- aller à la piscine.

   (A) préfèrent
   (B) rêvent
   (C) plaisent
   (D) insistent

7. Je ------- demande s'il est temps de partir.

   (A) elle
   (B) moi
   (C) se
   (D) vous

8. Les dames sont arrivées avec -------.

   (A) leur
   (B) il
   (C) eux
   (D) les

9. La voiture verte est -------.

   (A) les leurs
   (B) la vôtre
   (C) à aucun
   (D) ma

10. L'année dernière j'ai voyagé en -------.

    (A) Russie
    (B) États-Unis
    (C) New York
    (D) Canada

11. La réussite de ce projet est -------.

    (A) certainement
    (B) peu
    (C) probable
    (D) malgré

12. ------- ce soit fini.

    (A) Nous savons que
    (B) Il regrette que
    (C) Elle a oublié que
    (D) C'est lui qui a décidé que

13. C'est le collègue ------- j'ai beaucoup parlé.

    (A) dont
    (B) de quoi
    (C) sauf qui
    (D) avant que

14. ------- est le metteur en scène de ce film?

    (A) Quelle
    (B) Qu'est–ce qui
    (C) Où
    (D) Quoi

15. ------- avez-vous envie?

   (A) Quel
   (B) Y
   (C) Dont
   (D) De quoi

16. Le gouvernement ------- de négocier un accord.

   (A) va
   (B) espère
   (C) essaie
   (D) peut

17. ------- qu'il sache les nouvelles d'hier.

   (A) Sans doute
   (B) Je sais
   (C) Je crains
   (D) C'est à cause de Michel

18. Jean a réussi à trouver du travail ------- la grève.

   (A) afin de
   (B) lorsque
   (C) en dépit de
   (D) à moins de

19. -------, nous partirions.

   (A) Si elle en avait envie
   (B) Si tu peux
   (C) S'ils voudront
   (D) Si vous l'aviez permis

20. C'est le gâteau le plus délicieux -------.

   (A) que vous avez jamais mangé
   (B) qu'elle a jamais acheté
   (C) que nous avons jamais fait
   (D) que tu puisses jamais imaginer

Directions: The paragraphs below contain blank spaces indicating omissions in the text. For some blanks it is necessary to choose the completion that is most appropriate to the meaning of the passage; for other blanks, to choose the one completion that forms a grammatically correct sentence. In some instances, choice (A) may consist of dashes that indicate that no insertion is required to form a grammatically correct sentence. In each case, indicate your answer by filling in the corresponding oval on the answer sheet. Be sure to read each paragraph completely before answering the questions related to it.

Answers can be found on pages 100–102.

Si j'avais su, ------- aller avec Marie et Christine.

21.   (A) je pouvais
      (B) j'avais pu
      (C) je peux
      (D) j'aurais pu

Trop tard, j'ai essayé de ------- téléphoner

22.   (A) elles
      (B) leur
      (C) eux
      (D) la

chez ------- mais

23.   (A) elles
      (B) tu
      (C) leur
      (D) ils

------- n'était là.

24.   (A) personne
      (B) une personne
      (C) rien
      (D) nulle

-------, j'ai tenté de les retrouver au café.

25.   (A) Finalement
      (B) Terminé
      (C) Maintenant
      (D) Afin de

Quand ------- suis arrivé, je les ai

26. (A) j'en
    (B) j'y
    (C) je le
    (D) je me

------- entrer

27. (A) vu
    (B) vue
    (C) vus
    (D) vues

------- cinéma.

28. (A) à la
    (B) au
    (C) par la
    (D) par le

Avant ------- partir en vacances, Jean et Camille ont

29. (A) -------
    (B) à
    (C) de
    (D) que

------- à l'aéroport

30. (A) téléphoné
    (B) téléphonée
    (C) téléphonés
    (D) téléphonées

------- demander

31. (A) -------
    (B) à
    (C) de
    (D) pour

------- l'avion

32. (A) si
    (B) quand
    (C) quel
    (D) qui

partait -------.

33. (A) en temps
    (B) chaque heure
    (C) à l'heure
    (D) de temps en temps

EXPLANATIONS OF PRACTICE SECTIONS

If you have a particular question or concept, refer back to the section indicated.

Part B

1. Odds and Ends

   (A) *quelque chose* **is correct**
   (B) *rien* must be used with *ne—n'a rien*
   (C) *plusieurs* must modify something
   (D) *quelque* must modify something

2. Prepositions

   (A) *rejeter* cannot be followed by a verb
   (B) *aimer* takes the infinitive
   (C) *être obligé* **takes** *de,* **so it is correct**
   (D) *avoir voulu* takes the infinitive

3. Odds and Ends

   (A) plural
   (B) *amie* **is feminine, but it's correct because**
      amie **begins with a vowel**
   (C) feminine
   (D) plural

4. Odds and Ends

   (A) *avant de partir* **works with the future tense**
   (B) *tout à l'heure* is okay, but not with *à*
   (C) *hier* does not work with the future
   (D) *jamais* must be used with *ne*

5. Pronouns

   (A) *personne* requires *ne*
   (B) subject pronoun
   (C) indirect object
   (D) stressed pronoun is correct with *c'est*

6. Prepositions

   (A) *préférer* **takes the infinitive—correct**
   (B) *rêver* takes *de* and then the infinitive
   (C) *plaire* takes no direct object
   (D) *insister* takes *pour* and the infinitive

7. Pronouns

   (A) subject or stressed pronoun
   (B) stressed pronoun
   (C) reflexive, but wrong person
   (D) *demander quelque chose à quelqu'un—*
      indirect object is correct

8. Pronouns

   (A) indirect object pronoun
   (B) subject pronoun
   (C) stressed pronoun is correct with *avec* (see page 57)
   (D) direct object pronoun (see page 57)

9. Pronouns

   (A) plural
   (B) singular and feminine possessive pronoun—correct
   (C) *aucun* requires *ne*
   (D) possessive adjective

10. Prepositions

   (A) *Russie* is feminine—correct with *en*
   (B) *États-Unis* is plural *(aux)*
   (C) New York takes *à*
   (D) Canada is masculine *(au)*

11. Odds and Ends

   (A) adverb
   (B) adverb
   (C) adjective—correct
   (D) preposition

12. Verbs

   (A) *savoir que* doesn't take the subjunctive
   (B) *regretter que* takes the subjunctive—correct
   (C) *oublier que* doesn't take the subjunctive
   (D) nothing hypothetical, so no subjunctive

13. Pronouns/Prepositions

   (A) *parler* takes *de*—therefore *dont* is correct
   (B) *quoi* is used with things
   (C) *parler* cannot work with *sauf*
   (D) *avant que* is a conjunction, not a pronoun

14. Pronouns

   (A) *quelle* is feminine
   (B) *qu'est-ce qui* is used to refer to things
   (C) *Où* means "where"—correct
   (D) *quoi* is used with things

15. Pronouns

   (A) *quel* must modify something
   (B) *y* refers to place or location
   (C) *dont* cannot be used to begin a question
   (D) *avoir envie* takes *de*—correct

16. Prepositions

    (A) *aller* does not take *de*
    (B) *espérer* takes either the infinitive or *que*
    (C) *essayer* takes *de*—correct
    (D) *pouvoir* does not take *de*

17. Verbs

    (A) *sans doute* means "probably"
    (B) certain, so no subjunctive
    (C) *Je crains* means "I fear." This expression takes the subjunctive—correct
    (D) no doubt or uncertainty, so no subjunctive

18. Prepositions

    (A) in order to
    (B) when
    (C) in spite of—correct
    (D) unless

19. Verbs

    (A) imperfect followed by conditional—correct
    (B) present, so following clause can't be conditional
    (C) future cannot follow *si*
    (D) past imperfect would take past conditional

20. Verbs

    (A) *passé composé*
    (B) *passé composé*
    (C) *passé composé*
    (D) subjunctive is used with superlatives—correct

Part C

21. Verbs

    (A) imperfect
    (B) past imperfect
    (C) present
    (D) past conditional follows a clause with *si* and the past imperfect—correct

22. Pronouns

    (A) subject or stressed pronoun
    (B) indirect object—correct
    (C) stressed pronoun and masculine
    (D) direct object and singular

23. Pronouns

   (A) stressed pronoun with *chez*—correct
   (B) subject
   (C) indirect object
   (D) subject and masculine

24. Vocabulary

   (A) no one—correct
   (B) a person
   (C) nothing
   (D) *nulle* is an adjective

25. Vocabulary

   (A) Finally—correct
   (B) *Terminé* is not an adverb, but a past participle
   (C) Now
   (D) In order to

26. Pronouns

   (A) *arriver de* makes no sense in this context
   **(B) *y* indicates place, in this case the café—
       correct**
   (C) *le* is a direct object pronoun
   (D) *arriver* cannot be reflexive

27. Verbs

   (A) no agreement or masculine singular
   (B) feminine singular
   (C) masculine plural
   **(D) feminine plural: requires agreement because
       direct object precedes verb—correct**

28. Prepositions

   (A) *cinéma* is masculine
   (B) *au* is correct because *cinéma* is masculine
   (C) *entrer par* doesn't make sense in this context
       and *cinéma* is masculine
   (D) *entrer par* doesn't make sense in this context

29. Prepositions

   (A) you cannot use *avant* and a verb without a
       preposition
   (B) *avant à* does not exist
   (C) the correct expression is *avant de*
   (D) *avant que* would have to be followed by a
       clause using the subjunctive

30. Verbs

   (A) no agreement required—correct
   (B) feminine
   (C) masculine plural
   (D) feminine plural

31. Prepositions

   (A) needs a preposition to make sense
   (B) *à demander* makes no sense
   (C) *de demander* makes no sense
   (D) *pour demander*: to ask—correct

32. Conjunctions

   (A) *si*—correct
   (B) when
   (C) which
   (D) who

33. Vocabulary

   (A) *en temps* does not exist. *à temps* (on time)
        would be correct.
   (B) every hour
   (C) on time—correct
   (D) from time to time

6

Reading Comprehension

PART D: READING COMPREHENSION

The last section can have one of two formats. **In one format, there will be four to six passages** of 20 to 30 lines each. All the passages will be of a literary or journalistic nature. There will be roughly 26 questions in no clear order of difficulty.

In the other format, the reading comprehension passages will include one or two advertisement-type texts. If this is the case, you will have approximately thirty questions, again in no clear order of difficulty.

Here are the directions for this section as they appear on the test:

Part D

Directions: Read the following selections carefully for comprehension. Each selection is followed by a number of questions or incomplete statements. Select the completion or answer that is best according to the text and fill in the corresponding oval on the answer sheet.

WHAT IS THIS WEIRD TENSE?

In formal French, literary writing uses a tense called the *passé simple* (or past historic) instead of the *passé composé*. You don't need to know how to conjugate it or when to use it. You simply need to recognize which verb is being used.

Present	Past Participle	Passé Simple
il donne	donné	il donna
il croit	cru	il crut
il met	mis	il mit

PACING

This is the hardest section for most people. In addition, there is no clear order of difficulty. Short passages are not necessarily easier than long ones.

If you are fairly strong in vocabulary and grammar, this may be the place to skip a few questions. You'll probably want to do three of the four or four of the six, depending on the exact number of passages.

LITERARY/JOURNALISTIC PASSAGES

The passages are generally quite short. Read them through at a moderate pace to get a general idea of what the passage is about. Do not become obsessed if you don't understand every word or sentence.

THE QUESTIONS ARE IN ORDER

The first question will relate to the first sentence or two. Middle questions will refer to the middle of the passage. The answer to the last question will be found near the end.

GO BACK

Don't try to answer the questions based on your first reading of the passage. **Go back to the passage and reread the entire sentence or group of sentences that relate to the question.**

USE PROCESS OF ELIMINATION: POE

Common sense

You can eliminate answers that don't make sense in the context of the passage.

Familiar words — wrong context

Sometimes the words in an answer choice will be strongly reminiscent of the words used in the passage. If a word or phrase is directly lifted from the passage, be careful—you may be falling into a trap.

Misleading look-alikes

Sometimes, instead of repeating words verbatim, the College Board will take a word and twist it subtly. For example, if the word *errer* appears, they might have a trap answer choice containing the word *erreur*.

Try the following passage, looking for the types of trap answers mentioned above.

> La cité elle-même, on doit l'avouer, est laide.
> D'aspect tranquille, il faut quelque temps pour
> *Ligne* apercevoir ce qui la rend différente de tant d'autres
> villes commerçantes, sous toutes les latitudes. Com-
> (5) ment faire imaginer, par exemple, une ville sans pi-
> geons, sans arbres et sans jardins, où l'on ne rencon-
> tre ni battements d'ailes ni froissements de feuilles,
> un lieu neutre pour tout dire? Le changement des
> saisons ne s'y lit que dans le ciel. Le printemps
> (10) s'annonce seulement par la qualité de l'air ou par
> les corbeilles de fleurs que des petits vendeurs ramè-
> nent des banlieues; c'est un printemps qu'on vend
> sur les marchés. Pendant l'été, le soleil incendie les
> maisons trop sèches et couvre les murs d'une cendre
> (15) grise; on ne peut plus vivre alors que dans l'ombre
> des volets clos. En automne, c'est, au contraire, un
> déluge de boue. Les beaux jours viennent seulement
> en hiver.

(Camus, *La Peste*, Folio)

1. Ce passage nous décrit

   (A) une ville idéale
   (B) un marché en ville
   (C) les changements de saison
   (D) les attributs principaux d'une cité

The questions on reading comprehension go in order. The early questions relate to information early in the passage. Later questions refer to information that appears later in the passage.

The best way to get the right answer is to take the time to go back and carefully reread the sentence or sentences that relate to the question.

2. Qu'est-ce qui rend la cité différente des autres villes?

(A) La présence des pigeons
(B) La latitude
(C) Le manque de verdure et d'oiseaux
(D) La couleur du ciel

3. Aux lignes 13–14, "c'est un printemps qu'on vend sur les marchés" veut dire

(A) qu'on peut tout acheter au marché
(B) qu'on sait que le printemps est arrivé quand on peut acheter des fleurs
(C) qu'on voit mieux le printemps dans les banlieues
(D) que le printemps est comme un marché

Don't be afraid to eliminate answer choices that don't make sense.

4. Comment réagissent les habitants de la ville à l'arrivée de l'été?

(A) Ils font des feux.
(B) Ils se plaignent.
(C) Ils restent à l'intérieur.
(D) Ils deviennent des voleurs.

EXPLANATION OF PASSAGE

1. Ce passage nous décrit

(A) une ville idéale
(B) un marché en ville
(C) les changements de saisons
(D) les attributs principaux d'une cité

You are asked to choose what the passage describes:

(A) "an ideal town" is a misunderstanding of the first sentence. The first sentence tells us that the city is ugly, and the passage goes on to list primarily negative qualities. Eliminate this choice.

(B) "a marketplace in town" is an example of familiar words—wrong context. The word *marché* appears, as does the word *vendeurs*; however, the passage as a whole is not about the market. This choice is too specific. Eliminate it.

(C) "the changing of the seasons" is another example of familiar words—wrong context. The change of seasons is discussed, but again, it is too specific for this question.

(D) "the principal attributes of a town" is the correct answer. The passage discusses several distinctive features of a city.

2. Qu'est-ce qui rend la cité différente des autres villes?

(A) La présence des pigeons
(B) La latitude
(C) Le manque de verdure et d'oiseaux
(D) La couleur du ciel

You are asked to choose what makes the city different from others. The answer is in the section that starts with the second sentence of the passage.

(A) "the presence of pigeons" is an example of familiar words—wrong context. Pigeons are mentioned, but what is significant is their absence.

(B) "the latitude" is another example of familiar words—wrong context. The word "latitude" appears in the second sentence, but it is used to describe the location of other cities, in any latitude.

(C) "the lack of greenery and birds" is the correct answer. Notice that it paraphrases the third sentence: *sans pigeons, sans arbres et sans jardins.*

(D) "the color of the sky" takes the word *ciel* out of context. It is a misunderstanding of the sentence: *Le changement des saisons ne s'y lit que dans le ciel.* ("There, the change of season can only be seen in the color of the sky.")

Watch out for answers that use familiar words from the passage out of context.

3. Aux lignes 13–14, "c'est un printemps qu'on vend sur les marchés" veut dire

   (A) qu'on peut tout acheter au marché
   (B) qu'on sait que le printemps est arrivé quand on peut acheter des fleurs
   (C) qu'on voit mieux le printemps dans les banlieues
   (D) que le printemps est comme un marché

You are asked to interpret the sentence "it is a spring that is sold in the marketplace" within the context of the passage.

(A) "that one can buy everything at the market" is too literal and does not relate to the passage.

(B) "that one knows spring has arrived when one can buy flowers" is the correct answer. It corroborates the meaning, connecting it to the previous sentence about how few signs there are of the change of seasons.

(C) "that it is easier to see the spring in the suburbs" takes the word *banlieues* out of context.

(D) "that spring is like a marketplace" is a literal interpretation.

4. Comment réagissent les habitants de la ville à l'arrivée de l'été?

   (A) Ils font des feux.
   (B) Ils se plaignent.
   (C) Ils restent à l'intérieur.
   (D) Ils deviennent des voleurs.

"How do the inhabitants of the town react to the arrival of summer?" This topic is discussed in the next to last sentence of the passage.

(A) "They make fires" has a familiar word—wrong context.

(B) "They complain" comes out of the blue. Complaining is not discussed anywhere in the passage.

(C) "They stay indoors" is the correct answer. This is what the sentence "*on ne peut plus vivre alors que dans l'ombre des volets clos,*" implies—"then one can only live in the shade of closed shutters."

(D) "They become thieves" is an example of a misleading look-alike. Here the word *volets* (shutters) has been twisted into the word *voleurs.*

TICKETS/SCHEDULES/ADVERTISEMENTS

These graphical passages can be a blessing because you have less to read and because common sense works so well. **Pay special attention to the small print.**

- Read through the schedule or advertisement.

- Get a sense of the layout. Read all sizes of print.

- Use your common sense.

- Eliminate misleading look-alike words.

The Small Print

On ticket/schedule/ advertisement-type questions, pay special attention to the small print!

les jeunes aiment l'argent

Ils aiment l'argent signé Ravinet d'Enfert
Ravinet d'Enfert a créé, en métal argenté, une collection contemporaine de qualité. Héritier d'une longue tradition, éditeur d'une collection classique très réputée, Ravinet d'Enfert propose des créations de notre temps comme les services "Président" et "Brantôme." Ravinet d'Enfert les présente avec des couverts, des plats, des luminaires et des accessoires de table dans son catalogue "lignes actuelles."
Demandez-le dans les magasins ou à l'aide du bon à découper qui se trouve à droite.

RAVINET D'ENFERT
83, RUE DU TEMPLE—PARIS—3e

Veuillez m'adresser gratuitement vos catalogues
○ tradition
○ lignes actuelles

Nom _____
Prénom _____
Adresse _____

1. Selon la publicité, les services "Président" et "Brantôme"

   (A) sont d'une collection classique
   (B) coûtent beaucoup d'argent
   (C) sont très réputés
   (D) sont d'un style contemporain

2. Le bon à découper vous offre

   (A) des produits gratuits
   (B) un choix de catalogues
   (C) des adresses
   (D) une description de nouvelles lignes

EXPLANATION OF PASSAGE

1. Selon la publicité, les services "Président" et "Brantôme"

   (A) sont d'une collection classique
   (B) coûtent beaucoup d'argent
   (C) sont très réputés
   (D) sont d'un style contemporain

"According to the advertisement, the '*Président*' and '*Brantôme*' collections are . . ."

(A) "from a classic collection" takes a phrase out of context. The company produces a traditional line, but these styles, in contrast, are modern.

(B) "cost a lot of money" is also out of context. *Argent* is used here to mean "silver," not "money." This could be true, but there is no evidence of it in the ad.

(C) "have a good reputation" is also out of context. Again, the company is renowned, but we don't know about these specific lines.

(D) "are of a contemporary design" is the correct answer. Notice that it paraphrases the actual description *des créations de notre temps.*

2. Le bon à découper vous offre

   (A) des produits gratuits
   (B) un choix de catalogues
   (C) des adresses
   (D) une description de nouvelles lignes

"The coupon offers you . . ."

Le bon à découper vous offre refers to the coupon in the corner.

(A) "free products" is a familiar word, but it's in the wrong context. The catalog is free; the products are not.

(B) "a choice of catalogs" is the correct answer. The two boxes name two types of catalogs.

(C) "addresses" is a familiar word—wrong context. *Adresser* is part of a request to the company to send or address a catalog to the reader.

(D) "a description of new lines" is not terrible, but is not as good a choice (B). The coupon itself is not providing an actual description of the contemporary lines.

PRACTICE SECTION

Chez Rasseneur, après avoir mangé une soupe, Etienne, remonté dans l'étroite chambre qu'il allait oc-
Ligne cuper sous le toit, en face du Voreux, était tombé sur son lit, tout vêtu, assommé de fatigue. En deux jours,
(5) il n'avait pas dormi quatre heures. Quand il s'éveilla, au crépuscule, il resta étourdi un instant, sans reconnaître le lieu où il se trouvait; et il éprouvait un tel malaise, une telle pesanteur de tête, qu'il se mit péniblement debout, avec l'idée de prendre l'air, avant de dîner
(10) et de se coucher pour la nuit.

(Zola, *Germinal*, Garnier)

1. Etienne n'avait pas l'énergie de

   (A) dormir
   (B) se déshabiller
   (C) manger
   (D) mettre ses habits

2. Selon le passage, pour quelle raison Etienne est-il fatigué?

   (A) Il a trop mangé.
   (B) Il n'a pas dormi du tout depuis deux jours.
   (C) Il s'est couché à quatre heures du matin.
   (D) Il n'a dormi que quelques heures en 48 heures.

3. A quel moment de la journée s'est-il réveillé?

   (A) Tôt le matin
   (B) À midi
   (C) Tôt le soir
   (D) À minuit

4. Comment réagit-il au moment de se réveiller?

   (A) Il ne se souvient pas où il est.
   (B) Il ne trouve pas ses habits.
   (C) Il se sent en retard.
   (D) Il a faim.

5. Que voulait-il faire avant de dîner?

   (A) Respirer
   (B) Se promener
   (C) S'éveiller
   (D) Courir

Ligne

Chaque dimanche, avant la guerre, Morissot partait dès l'aurore, une canne en bambou d'une main, une boîte en fer-blanc sur le dos. Il prenait le chemin de fer d'Argenteuil, descendait à Colombes, puis (5) gagnait à pied l'île Marante. A peine arrivé en ce lieu de ses rêves, il se mettait à pêcher; il pêchait jusqu'à la nuit.

Chaque dimanche, il rencontrait là un petit homme replet et jovial, M. Sauvage, mercier, rue (10) Notre-Dame-de-Lorette, un autre pêcheur fanatique. Ils passaient souvent une demi-journée à côté, la ligne à la main et les pieds ballants au-dessus du courant; et ils s'étaient pris d'amitié l'un pour l'autre.

(Guy de Maupassant, *Deux Amis*, Le Livre de Poche)

6. Quand Morissot partait-il pour l'île?

   (A) Après le coucher du soleil
   (B) Au moment du coucher du soleil
   (C) Au moment du lever du soleil
   (D) L'après-midi

7. Comment gagnait-il l'île?

   (A) En autobus et à pied
   (B) En bateau
   (C) En voiture et à pied
   (D) En train et à pied

8. A quel moment commençait-il à pêcher?

   (A) Pratiquement au moment où il arrivait
   (B) Au moment où il commençait à rêver
   (C) À la tombée de la nuit
   (D) Quand son ami arrivait

9. Qu'est-ce qui se trouvait dans la rue Notre-Dame-de-Lorette?

   (A) L'île Marante
   (B) L'endroit où les deux amis se rencontraient
   (C) Le magasin de M. Sauvage
   (D) La gare

Claire.—Tes parents t'interdisent-ils d'aller voir un film?

Ligne
Guillaume.—Non, puisque je leur demande ce qu'ils en pensent. Quelquefois, ils me disent: "Il vaut (5) mieux que tu ailles voir un autre film."

Claire.—Moi, mes parents pensent qu'à mon âge, le cinéma n'est pas très bon, de toute façon.

Gilles.—Tu n'y vas jamais, alors?

Claire.—Si, mais en cachette.

(10) **Guillaume.**—Ça alors, moi je ne le ferai jamais . . . Je ne peux pas mentir à mes parents. Je crois que je me sens libre parce que mes parents pensent que c'est un peu à moi de choisir, mais pas n'importe quoi.

(*Pour ou contre*, Hachette)

10. Les parents de Guillaume

   (A) lui conseillent de ne jamais aller au cinéma
   (B) ne sont pas concernés par ce qu'il fait
   (C) n'aiment pas le cinéma
   (D) lui donnent leur avis sur les films qu'il choisit

11. A la question de Gilles, Claire répond

   (A) qu'elle ne va jamais au cinéma
   (B) qu'elle va au cinéma si ses parents sont d'accord
   (C) qu'elle va au cinéma sans le dire à ses parents
   (D) qu'elle va souvent au cinéma

12. Quelle raison Guillaume donne-t-il pour ne pas mentir à ses parents?

   (A) Ses parents le laissent faire n'importe quoi.
   (B) Ses parents lui donnent la responsabilité de décider que faire.
   (C) Il vaut mieux ne pas le faire.
   (D) Ses parents n'aiment pas le cinéma.

Attention! Dans le 5e, le boulevard Saint-Michel et la place Saint-André-des-Arts ne sont plus fréquentables! Les petits bars sympathiques et les restaurants à petits prix ont disparu au profit d'établissements prétentieux où un personnel pressé sert des bières à la chaîne. On débite des sandwiches sous cellophane, des frites et, signe des temps, McDonald et Wimpy se font face, à deux pas du Luxembourg. Cinémas et librairies semblent résister, pour l'instant, à cette invasion "made in U.S." Les jeunes se pressent chez "Gibert" et dans les salles d'art et d'essai où passent les vieux films d'hier et ceux d'avant-garde. Pour se rencontrer, les jeunes préfèrent les petites rues plus anonymes, les petits restaurants à six ou sept tables, les bars sans faux clinquant que l'on trouve autour du Panthéon.

Ligne (5), (10), (15) denote line markers.

(*Paris*, Hachette)

13. L'auteur réagit au changement sur le boulevard Saint-Michel et sur la place Saint-André-des-Arts avec

   (A) impatience
   (B) regret
   (C) indifférence
   (D) plaisir

14. Qu'est-ce qu'on trouve près du Luxembourg?

   (A) Des petits restaurants anonymes
   (B) Des cafés sympathiques
   (C) Des librairies prétentieuses
   (D) Des établissements américains

15. D'après le passage, on comprend que "Gibert" est

   (A) un film
   (B) un café
   (C) une librairie
   (D) un musée

16. Que font les jeunes au lieu d'aller boulevard Saint-Michel?

   (A) Ils fréquentent la place Saint-André-des-Arts.
   (B) Ils sont pressés d'aller voir des films américains.
   (C) Ils cherchent des bars sympathiques dans un autre endroit.
   (D) Ils résistent à l'envie d'aller dans les librairies.

Je n'ai rien à cacher. J'étais orpheline et pauvre, j'élevais mon frère cadet. Un vieil ami de mon père m'a demandé ma main. Il était riche et bon, j'ai accepté. Qu'auriez-vous fait à ma place? Mon frère était malade et sa santé réclamait les plus grands soins. J'ai vécu six ans avec mon mari sans un nuage. Il y a deux ans, j'ai rencontré celui que je devais aimer. Nous nous sommes reconnus tout de suite, il voulait que je parte avec lui et j'ai refusé.

(Sartre, *Huis-clos*, Folio)

17. La narratrice donne à entendre qu'elle

   (A) travaillait beaucoup
   (B) était invalide
   (C) avait beaucoup de soucis
   (D) s'était mariée avec l'ami de son père

18. Le frère de la narratrice

   (A) a vécu avec elle pendant six ans
   (B) était plus jeune qu'elle
   (C) était soldat
   (D) n'aimait pas son mari

19. Le passage nous donne l'impression

   (A) qu'elle voulait défendre ses actions
   (B) que son mari lui manquait
   (C) que son frère était guéri
   (D) qu'elle aimait le beau temps

20. Après six ans, qu'est-ce qui s'est passé?

   (A) Le mari de la narratrice est parti.
   (B) Le beau temps a changé.
   (C) La narratrice a décidé de partir.
   (D) La narratrice a trouvé un amant.

Antoine Lemurier, qui avait manqué mourir, sortit heureusement de maladie, reprit son service au bureau, et, tant bien que mal, pansa ses plaies d'argent. Durant cette épreuve, les voisins s'étaient

(5) réjouis en pensant que le mari allait crever, le mobilier être vendu, la femme à la rue. Tous étaient d'ailleurs d'excellentes gens, des cœurs d'or, comme tout le monde, et n'en voulaient nullement au ménage Lemurier, mais voyant se jouer auprès d'eux

(10) une sombre tragédie avec rebonds, péripéties, beuglements de proprio, huissier et fièvre montante, ils vivaient anxieusement dans l'attente d'un dénouement qui fût digne de la pièce.

(Marcel Aymé, *Les Sabines*, Folio)

21. On comprend qu'Antoine Lemurier

   (A) est mort
   (B) a raté le train
   (C) a quitté son bureau
   (D) a failli succomber à une maladie

22. Qu'est-ce que les voisins pensaient de la maladie de Lemurier?

   (A) Ils attendaient une fin intéressante à la tragédie.
   (B) Ils étaient tristes.
   (C) Ils étaient fâchés contre Lemurier.
   (D) Ils tombaient malades.

23. Selon les voisins, qu'est-ce qui serait "un dénouement . . . digne" de la situation?

   (A) M. Lemurier perd son travail.
   (B) M. Lemurier récupère complètement.
   (C) Mme Lemurier est sans abri.
   (D) Mme Lemurier vend la maison.

EXPLANATION OF PRACTICE SECTION
Part D

1. Etienne lacked the energy to

   (A) "sleep": familiar word—wrong context
   (B) "undress": see phrase *tout vêtu* (fully dressed)
   (C) "eat"
   (D) "put on his clothes"

2. According to the passage, why is Etienne tired?

   (A) "He ate too much." familiar words—wrong context
   (B) "He did not sleep at all in two days." Too extreme; he did get some sleep.
   (C) "He went to sleep at four in the morning." familiar words—wrong context
   (D) "He has slept only for a few hours in 48 hours": See *En deux jours, il n'avait pas dormi quatre heures.*

3. At what time of day did he get up?

   (A) "early in the morning"
   (B) "noon"
   (C) "early in the evening": See *au crépuscule, avant de . . . se coucher pour la nuit.*
   (D) "midnight"

4. How does he react at the moment he wakes up?

   (A) "He doesn't remember where he is": See *sans reconnaître le lieu où il se trouvait.*
   (B) "He can't find his clothes."
   (C) "He feels that he is late."
   (D) "He is hungry."

5. What did he want to do before eating dinner?

   (A) "breathe"
   (B) "go for a walk": See *prendre l'air*
   (C) "wake up": familiar words—wrong context
   (D) "run"

6. When did Morissot leave to reach the island?

   (A) "after sunset"
   (B) "at sunset"
   (C) "at sunrise": See *dès l'aurore*
   (D) "in the afternoon"

7. How did he reach the island?

   (A) "by bus and on foot"
   (B) "by boat"
   (C) "by car and on foot"
   (D) "by train and on foot": See *chemin de fer*
       (railway), *à pied*

8. At what point did he start fishing?

   (A) "at almost the moment he arrived": See *à*
       peine arrivé
   (B) "at the moment he started to dream"
   (C) "at nightfall"
   (D) "when his friend arrived"

9. What is located on Notre-Dame-de-Lorrette Street?

   (A) "the island": makes no sense
   (B) "the place the two friends would meet"
   (C) "Mr. Savage's shop": See *mercier* **(dealer in**
       sewing wares)
   (D) "the train station"

---

10. The parents of Guillaume

    (A) "advise him never to go to the movies"
    (B) "don't concern themselves with what he
        does"
    (C) "don't like the movies"
    (D) "give their opinion about the films he
        chooses": See *je leur demande ce qu'ils en*
        pensent.

11. To Gilles's question, Claire replies

    (A) "that she never goes to the movies"
    (B) "that she goes to the movies if her parents
        agree"
    (C) "that she goes to the movies without telling
        her parents": see *en cachette* **(secretly)**
    (D) "that she goes to the movies often"

12. What reason does Guillaume give for not lying to
    his parents?

    (A) "His parents let him do anything.": familiar
        words—wrong context
    (B) "His parents let him decide what to do":
        See *Je crois que je me sens libre*
    (C) "It is better not to do it."
    (D) "His parents don't like the movies."

---

13. The author reacts to the change with

    (A) "impatience"
    (B) "regret"
    (C) "indifference"
    (D) "pleasure": makes no sense

14. What does one find near the Luxembourg Gardens?

    (A) "small, anonymous restaurants": familiar words—wrong context
    (B) "pleasant cafés": familiar words—wrong context
    (C) "pretentious bookstores"
    (D) "American establishments": *McDonald's et Wimpy*

15. According to the passage, "Gibert" is

    (A) "a film"
    (B) "a café"
    (C) "a bookstore": See *cinémas et librairies semblent résister*
    (D) "a museum"

16. What do young people do instead of going to Boulevard St. Michel?

    (A) "They go to Place Saint-André-des-Arts."
    (B) "They are in a rush to see American films."
    (C) "They look for cool bars in another area.": See *autour du Panthéon*
    (D) "They resist going to bookstores."

---

17. The narrator lets it be understood that she

    (A) "worked a lot"
    (B) "was an invalid"
    (C) "had many worries"
    (D) "married her father's friend": See *Un vieil ami de mon père m'a demandé ma main.*

18. The brother of the narrator

    (A) "lived with her for six years": familiar words—wrong context
    (B) *cadet*: **"was younger than she"**
    (C) "was a soldier"
    (D) "didn't like her husband"

19. The passage gives us the impression

   (A) "that she wanted to defend her actions":
       See *Qu'auriez-vous fait à ma place?*
   (B) "that she missed her husband"
   (C) "that her brother was cured"
   (D) "that she liked good weather"
       misunderstanding as *sans un nuage* is not
       literal

20. After six years, what happened?

   (A) "The husband of the narrator left."
   (B) "The good weather changed.": *sans un nuage*
       is not literal
   (C) "The narrator decided to leave."
   (D) "The narrator found a lover.": See *j'ai*
       rencontré celui que je devais aimer.

---

21. It is understood that Antoine Lemurier

   (A) "is dead"
   (B) "missed the train"
   (C) "left his work"
   (D) "nearly succumbed to an illness": See *avait*
       ***manqué mourir* (almost died)**

22. What did the neighbors think of Lemurier's illness?

   (A) "They expected an interesting end to the
       tragedy.": See *ils vivaient anxieusement*
       dans l'attente d'un dénouement qui fût
       digne de la pièce.
   (B) "They were sad."
   (C) "They were angry with Lemurier."
   (D) "They fell ill."

23. According to the neighbors, what would have been
    a dignified end to the situation?

   (A) "Mr. Lemurier loses his job."
   (B) "Mr. Lemurier completely recovers."
   (C) "Mrs. Lemurier is without shelter.": See *la*
       femme à la rue.
   (D) "Mrs. Lemurier sells the house.": Close, but
       the phrase is *le mobilier allait être vendu*

7

French Listening

The SAT French Test with Listening is currently administered only in November at participating schools and requires a special registration form. There are currently no plans to offer the test more frequently.

OVERALL STRUCTURE OF THE LISTENING TEST

The SAT French Subject Test with Listening consists of **40 minutes of reading (written questions)** and **20 minutes of listening (oral questions)**, with 85 to 90 questions in all. This means that about two-thirds of the SAT French Subject Test with Listening consists of questions we've already discussed. You will have 40 minutes to work on those. There are, however, fewer of each type.

The French Listening test is two-thirds the question types reviewed in the preceding chapters and one-third listening questions.

- Part A—Vocabulary Completions: 12–16 questions
- Part B—Grammar Blanks: 12–16 questions
- Part C—Paragraph Blanks: 8 questions
- Part D—Reading Comprehension: 20–25 questions

In addition to those regular questions, you will have 20 minutes to work on the listening part of the test. There will be three parts with a total of about 40 questions covering pictures (8–12 questions); dialogues (10–12 questions); and monologues (10–15 questions):

- Listening—Part A: Pictures
- Listening—Part B: Short Dialogues and Monologues
- Listening—Part C: Longer Dialogues and Monologues

Samples of each type of question are available on the College Board's website, www.collegeboard.com.

SHOULD YOU SIGN UP FOR THE
FRENCH SUBJECT TEST WITH LISTENING?

Unless your comprehension of French is very strong or unless one of your schools requires it, probably not. As described above, most of the Listening Section is entirely aural; except in Part C, you have no written questions or answers to refer to. If you get stuck on one question, it can throw you off for the rest of that question type. You can't take extra time on a question or skip one and go back to it. You must follow the pace of the tape.

The SAT French with Listening benefits students with substantial experience speaking and listening to French (i.e., students who have spent a year abroad or whose knowledge of French comes from living in a French-speaking country or in a French-speaking home). The Listening test might also be easier for students who are very weak in grammar and reading comprehension but who have a good ear for the language. The Listening questions are easier in content than the regular questions, and there are proportionately fewer grammar and reading questions.

LISTENING—PART A: PHOTOS

The first part of the Listening Test consists of choosing which spoken phrase best matches the provided photo. Each sentence will be designated (A), (B), (C), or (D).

> Directions: For each item in this part, you will hear four sentences designated (A), (B), (C), and (D). They will not be printed in your test booklet. As you listen, look at the picture in your test booklet and select the choice that best reflects what you see in the picture or what someone in the picture might say. Then fill in the corresponding oval on the answer sheet. You will hear the choices only once. Now look at the following example.

Look at the picture before the answer choices are played. Get a general idea of what is going on.

MAKE A DECISION AS YOU HEAR EACH CHOICE

As each answer choice is read to you, decide if that choice is at all appropriate. If it is not, cross out that choice on your answer sheet. You may not be allowed to write in your book. If the choice is good or possible, make a mark inside the bubble. Probably only one will make any sense. If not, guess. **Don't wait to hear all the choices before deciding about each of them.** Erase all stray marks once you select an answer.

LISTENING—PART B: DIALOGUES

On this section you will hear a dialogue between two people, or a monologue. The initial selection will be repeated. It will be followed by three answer choices labeled (A), (B), or (C). The answer choices will be heard only once.

> Directions: In this part of the test you will hear several short selections. A tone will announce each new selection. The selections will not be printed in your test booklet, but each will be repeated. At the end of each selection, you will be asked one or two questions about what was said, each followed by three possible answers, (A), (B), and (C). The answers are not printed in your test booklet. You will hear them only once. Select the best answer and fill in the corresponding oval on the answer sheet. Now listen to the following example, but do not mark the answer on your answer sheet.

MAKE A DECISION AS YOU HEAR EACH CHOICE

As you hear each answer choice, decide if it is appropriate or not. Eliminate it or keep it on your answer sheet. Once you've selected an answer, erase all stray marks. Do not mark (D) or (E) as choices.

Now Hear This

The tricky thing about SAT French with Listening is that you must go at the pace of the tape, not your own pace.

LISTENING — PART C: LONG PASSAGES

This section consists of longer monologues or dialogues that will be heard only once. In this section the questions and the answer choices will be in the test booklet.

HEAR YE, HEAR YE

On Part C of the listening part of the test, answer the questions as you hear the information being presented. Don't wait to hear the whole thing!

> Directions: You will now hear some extended dialogues. You will hear each only once. After each dialogue, you will be asked several questions about what you have just heard. These questions are also printed in your test booklet. Select the best answer to each question from among the four choices printed in your test booklet and fill in the corresponding oval on the answer sheet. There is no sample question for this part.

FOREWARNED, FOREARMED

The great thing about this question type in Part C is that the questions and answer choices are printed in your booklet. As the instructions are being read (familiarize yourself with them now so that you already know them) and before the passage is read, read the questions and their answers to get a sense of the topic.

As in reading comprehension, the questions are in chronological order. Don't wait for the entire passage to be read before answering the questions. (It would be hard for even a native speaker to remember all those details for so long.) As the passage is being read, look at each question and mark the correct answer as soon as you hear it. The questions will either ask you to repeat specific details or paraphrase them. You are not required to interpret or infer.

PART ◆ III

The Princeton Review Practice SAT French Subject Tests and Explanations

8

Practice SAT French Subject Test 1

FRENCH SUBJECT TEST 1

SECTION 1

Your responses to the SAT French questions must be filled in on Section 1 of your answer sheet (at the back of the book). Marks on any other section will not be counted toward your score.

When your supervisor gives the signal, turn the page and begin the SAT French Subject Test. There are 100 numbered ovals on the answer sheet and 85 questions in the SAT French Subject Test. Therefore, use only ovals 1 to 85 for recording your answers.

FRENCH SUBJECT TEST 1

PLEASE NOTE THAT YOUR ANSWER SHEET HAS FIVE ANSWER POSITIONS MARKED A, B, C, D, E, WHILE THE QUESTIONS THROUGHOUT THIS TEST CONTAIN ONLY FOUR CHOICES. BE SURE <u>NOT</u> TO MAKE ANY MARKS IN COLUMN E.

Part A

<u>Directions:</u> This part consists of a number of incomplete statements, each having four suggested completions. Select the most appropriate completion and fill in the corresponding oval on the answer sheet.

---

1. Je dois faire ma . . . avant de partir en vacances demain.

   (A) bouche
   (B) voiture
   (C) valise
   (D) faute

2. Il fait beau dehors, veux-tu te . . . après le dîner?

   (A) laver
   (B) demander
   (C) lever
   (D) promener

3. Le soldat attendait avec impatience la fin de . . .

   (A) la route
   (B) la gare
   (C) la guerre
   (D) l'immeuble

4. Il est interdit de garder vos chaussures dans la maison; laissez-les . . .

   (A) de plus
   (B) d'accord
   (C) d'habitude
   (D) dehors

5. Paul a besoin d' . . . pour soutenir son pantalon.

   (A) un bras
   (B) une poche
   (C) une jambe
   (D) une ceinture

6. Pour son anniversaire, le garçon a reçu plusieurs . . .

   (A) jours
   (B) talents
   (C) jardins
   (D) cadeaux

7. J'ai acheté . . . dans la boulangerie d'à côté.

   (A) des fruits
   (B) du pain
   (C) de la viande
   (D) du boulot

8. Le . . . de mon immeuble est 564.

   (A) nombre
   (B) guide
   (C) numéro
   (D) nom

GO ON TO THE NEXT PAGE ➤

9. Il y a douze . . . dans un an.

   (A) mois
   (B) jours
   (C) heures
   (D) saisons

10. Le cinéma est vide; nous pouvons nous . . . n'importe où.

    (A) endormir
    (B) articuler
    (C) assister
    (D) asseoir

11. Quand je porte mes souliers préférés, je n'ai jamais mal aux . . .

    (A) coudes
    (B) pieds
    (C) lèvres
    (D) oreilles

12. Je suis d'accord avec lui; je pense qu'il a . . .

    (A) tort
    (B) raison
    (C) mal
    (D) nécessité

13. Mon bureau se trouve dans un . . . différent de mon appartement.

    (A) quartier
    (B) gazon
    (C) voyage
    (D) plan

14. Le héros a . . . une fille qui était en train de se noyer.

    (A) sauvé
    (B) nagé
    (C) remercié
    (D) traîné

15. L'été, il faut porter des . . . de soleil pour se protéger les yeux.

    (A) spectacles
    (B) cheveux
    (C) lunettes
    (D) rayons

16. Il faut faire attention avant de . . . la rue.

    (A) traverser
    (B) transpirer
    (C) traduire
    (D) transformer

17. Ce n'est pas gentil de . . . tes amis.

    (A) lire
    (B) remplir
    (C) taquiner
    (D) tolérer

18. Le bruit constant m' . . .

    (A) énerve
    (B) enseigne
    (C) enlève
    (D) enferme

GO ON TO THE NEXT PAGE

19. Le serveur a . . . mon verre de vin.

    (A) rempli
    (B) reculé
    (C) remonté
    (D) revu

20. La dame a . . . le bras pour attraper le ballon.

    (A) tendu
    (B) renversé
    (C) retiré
    (D) perdu

21. L'étudiant a écrit . . . sur les oeuvres de Maupassant.

    (A) une boulette
    (B) une recette
    (C) une dissertation
    (D) un témoin

22. Sans la protection d'un parapluie, je vais être . . . par la pluie.

    (A) tenté
    (B) trempé
    (C) tendu
    (D) tempéré

23. Les trains passent moins souvent les jours . . .

    (A) normaux
    (B) libres
    (C) fériés
    (D) courants

24. Les alpinistes vont . . . l'ascension du Mont Kilimandjaro.

    (A) modifier
    (B) montrer
    (C) tirer
    (D) tenter

25. Des années d'usage vont . . . le cuir de ces bottes.

    (A) assiéger
    (B) réduire
    (C) assouplir
    (D) surprendre

26. Si je pars maintenant, je peux . . . l'heure d'affluence.

    (A) estimer
    (B) revoir
    (C) arranger
    (D) éviter

GO ON TO THE NEXT PAGE

FRENCH SUBJECT TEST 1—*Continued*

Part B

<u>Directions:</u> Each of the following sentences contains a blank. From the four choices given, select the one that can be inserted in the blank to form a grammatically correct sentence and fill in the corresponding oval on the answer sheet. Choice (A) may consist of dashes that indicate that no insertion is required to form a grammatically correct sentence.

---

27. Le monsieur ------- à vous suggérer.

    (A) n'a quelque chose
    (B) n'a pas
    (C) n'a rien
    (D) a rien

28. À ------- est ce manteau vert?

    (A) que
    (B) qui
    (C) lequel
    (D) quoi

29. J'aime beaucoup cet -------.

    (A) homme
    (B) huile d'olive
    (C) dame
    (D) livre

30. Aimez-vous la plage? Nous ------- allons après la classe.

    (A) en
    (B) où
    (C) y
    (D) là

31. La semaine prochaine je visite ma cousine à -------.

    (A) Mexique
    (B) France
    (C) Paris
    (D) Chine

32. Elle a ------- perdu ses clés.

    (A) fréquent
    (B) jamais
    (C) souvent
    (D) probable

33. Jean-Claude est venu avec -------.

    (A) ils
    (B) leur
    (C) eux
    (D) soi

34. C'est une décision ------- laquelle je vais beaucoup réfléchir.

    (A) à
    (B) sans
    (C) avec
    (D) dont

35. C'est lui qui ------- vendu la voiture.

    (A) a
    (B) est
    (C) aie
    (D) soit

36. Je ------- l'avis de mon ami.

    (A) m'excuse
    (B) résiste
    (C) considère
    (D) réfléchis

GO ON TO THE NEXT PAGE

37. Pierre ------- dehors quand le téléphone a sonné.

    (A) est
    (B) était
    (C) soit
    (D) serait

38. Si Paul achetait un journal, il ------- déjà les résultats.

    (A) savait
    (B) aurait su
    (C) saura
    (D) saurait

39. ------- les mains avant de manger!

    (A) Lavez
    (B) Brossez-vous
    (C) Serrez
    (D) Lavez-vous

40. Il n'a pas ------- signer les papiers.

    (A) décidé
    (B) le droit
    (C) envie
    (D) voulu

41. Il faut que tu ------- attention avant de traverser la rue.

    (A) fasses
    (B) fais
    (C) feras
    (D) faisais

42. C'est à cause de ------- que nous avons raté le train.

    (A) il
    (B) moi
    (C) se
    (D) leur

43. Est-ce que ------- cette dame qui va nous montrer la chambre?

    (A) c'est
    (B) ce soit
    (C) c'était
    (D) sera

44. Mon travail est ------- que le vôtre.

    (A) si difficile
    (B) le meilleur
    (C) pire
    (D) trop

45. Nous avons beaucoup progressé ------- l'époque du Professeur LeBlanc.

    (A) durant
    (B) sinon
    (C) afin de
    (D) avant que

46. ------- m'a écrit.

    (A) Celui qui
    (B) Tu
    (C) C'est lui qui
    (D) Personne

GO ON TO THE NEXT PAGE →

Part C

Directions: The paragraphs below contain blank spaces indicating omissions in the text. For some blanks it is necessary to choose the completion that is most appropriate to the meaning of the passage; for other blanks, to choose the one completion that forms a grammatically correct sentence. In some instances, choice (A) may consist of dashes that indicate that no insertion is required to form a grammatically correct sentence. In each case, indicate your answer by filling in the corresponding oval on the answer sheet. Be sure to read the paragraph completely before answering the questions related to it.

Il est trois heures et demie du matin quand j' ------- avec ma femme,

47. (A) arrivais
    (B) arriverais
    (C) arrive
    (D) étais arrivé

sur le terrain de l'aérodrome pour le grand départ. Après avoir -------

48. (A) attendu
    (B) attendue
    (C) attendus
    (D) attendues

pendant plusieurs jours un temps ------- , nous sommes ------- prêts à

49. (A) passé   50. (A) loin d'être
    (B) mauvais   (B) jamais
    (C) triste   (C) enfin
    (D) favorable   (D) simplement

partir ------- Tokyo.

51. (A) dans
    (B) sans
    (C) en
    (D) pour

Trois ou quatre cents personnes sont là pour ------- à notre

52. (A) assister
    (B) assommer
    (C) asseoir
    (D) aspirer

GO ON TO THE NEXT PAGE ➤

envol. Je ne sais pas comment cela se fait, ------- que nous n'avions dit à

53. (A) malgré
    (B) parce
    (C) sans
    (D) dès

personne que nous partions.

Je suis très -------, mais notre avion est très chargé et la piste

54. (A) fière
    (B) énervé
    (C) calme
    (D) lourd

est couverte d'herbe. Je connais bien les dangers qu'il y a à ------- dans

55. (A) débarrasser
    (B) déborder
    (C) développer
    (D) décoller

ces conditions. Tout a été longuement -------, discuté entre nous depuis

56. (A) étudié
    (B) étudier
    (C) étude
    (D) étudiant

des-------, avec une très grande attention. Maintenant,

57. (A) minutes
    (B) secondes
    (C) moments
    (D) semaines

j' ------- l'esprit tranquille.

58. (A) ai
    (B) avais
    (C) aurais
    (D) ai été

GO ON TO THE NEXT PAGE

Part D

<u>Directions</u>: Read the following texts carefully for comprehension. Each is followed by a number of questions or incomplete statements. Select the completion or answer that is best according to the text and fill in the corresponding oval on the answer sheet.

Ayant laissé la voiture au garage, ils décidèrent d'attendre dans un café. Les longues files de maisons qui s'étendaient de chaque côté de la route ne formaient pas un village.
Ligne C'était plutôt comme un faubourg lointain de Chartres,
(5) avec des maisons basses, et çà et là une devanture terne d'épicerie de campagne. Deux enfants couraient l'un après l'autre. On entendait quelqu'un frapper régulièrement une pièce de métal dans un atelier voisin. Ils se dirigèrent vers le café le plus proche. C'était l'heure creuse. Il n'y
(10) avait personne. Un chat dormait sur le comptoir. Le patron apparut au bout de quelques instants, comme à regret, en traînant les jambes. Ils commandèrent n'importe quoi pour justifier leur présence. Pendant qu'il les servait, elle avait tiré un poudrier de son sac et vérifiait son maquillage,
(15) machinalement. Elle était engourdie, un peu dolente, comme si on l'eût enveloppée dans une couche épaisse de coton, et les bruits ne lui parvenaient qu'assourdis. Peut-être la fatigue du voyage.

(Jean Forgère, *La Panne*, Le Livre de Poche)

59. Qu'est-ce que le couple a fait avant de chercher le café?

   (A) Ils ont attendu.
   (B) Ils ont emmené leur automobile à un garage.
   (C) Ils ont parlé avec deux enfants.
   (D) Ils ont frappé quelque chose.

60. Où se trouve le couple?

   (A) À Chartres
   (B) Dans un village
   (C) Dans une grande ville
   (D) Dans la banlieue d'une ville

61. Quelle est la raison pour laquelle le couple est venu au café?

   (A) Pour manger un bon repas
   (B) Pour trouver quelqu'un avec qui ils pourraient parler
   (C) Pour demander leur chemin
   (D) Pour passer le temps

62. Qu'est-ce que l'auteur veut dire par l'expression "l'heure creuse"?

   (A) Qu'il y avait beaucoup de monde dans le café
   (B) Qu'il faisait presque nuit
   (C) Que personne n'était là
   (D) Que c'était l'heure où le café fermait

63. Quelle impression avait la dame au café?

   (A) Qu'elle avait mangé du coton
   (B) Qu'elle était trop maquillée
   (C) Qu'il y avait trop de bruit
   (D) Qu'elle entendait mal

GO ON TO THE NEXT PAGE

Il y a, au fond de beaucoup de Français, un champion de course automobile qui sommeille et que réveille le simple contact du pied sur l'accélérateur. Le citoyen paisible, *Ligne* qui vous a obligeamment invité à prendre place dans sa (5) voiture, peut se métamorphoser sous vos yeux en pilote démoniaque. Jérôme Charnelet, ce bon père de famille, qui n'écraserait pas une mouche contre une vitre, est tout prêt à écraser un piéton au kilomètre, pourvu qu'il se sente "dans son droit." Au signal vert, il voit rouge. Rien ne l'arrête (10) plus, pas même le jaune. Sur la route, cet homme, qui passe pour rangé, ne se range pas du tout. Ce n'est qu'à bout de ressources, et après avoir subi une klaxonnade nourrie, qu'il consentira de mauvaise grâce à abandonner le milieu de la chaussée.

(*L'Auto*, Hachette)

64. L'auteur écrit dans un style

    (A) sérieux
    (B) neutre
    (C) drôle
    (D) scientifique

65. Qu'est-ce qui fait apparaître le "champion de course automobile"?

    (A) L'action de se mettre au volant de l'automobile
    (B) Le lever du soleil
    (C) L'action de se réveiller
    (D) Un klaxon

66. D'après le passage, Jérôme Charnelet est d'habitude

    (A) un champion de course
    (B) d'une disposition aimable
    (C) impatient
    (D) généreux

67. Comment Jérôme réagit-il au signal vert?

    (A) Il s'arrête.
    (B) Il écrase une mouche.
    (C) Il ne réussit pas à voir les couleurs.
    (D) Il devient un conducteur démoniaque.

68. D'après le passage, qu'est-ce qui convaincrait Jérôme de changer de position sur la chaussée?

    (A) La réalisation qu'il est au milieu de la route
    (B) Son sens de ses obligations envers les autres conducteurs
    (C) Les klaxons des autres conducteurs
    (D) La couleur du signal

69. On comprend que Jérôme conduit d'une manière

    (A) ordonnée
    (B) rangée
    (C) gracieuse
    (D) obsédée

GO ON TO THE NEXT PAGE →

92 HAUTS DE SEINE
Le confort du neuf, le charme de l'ancien

Résidence "Le Valvert." Aux portes de Paris et près d'un accès autoroutier, dans immeuble du XIXe siècle, 10 appartements en cours de rénovation (du studio au 4 pièces). Parking privé dans cour intérieure. Proche du centre ville avec vue exceptionnelle sur parc aux arbres centenaires.

Prix à partir de 110000

Livraison 3ème trimestre 2005.
Bureau de vente et appartement-témoin:
01 587 45 35 12

Du lundi au samedi de 9 h 30 à 19 h, le dimanche uniquement sur rendez-vous.

70. Ces appartements
    (A) vont être rénovés en 2005
    (B) ont été rénovés au XIXe siècle
    (C) sont en train d'être rénovés
    (D) sont rénovés

71. Cette publicité s'adresse à
    (A) des acheteurs éventuels
    (B) de futurs locataires
    (C) des personnes âgées
    (D) des vendeurs

72. Après avoir lu cette publicité, on connaît tout SAUF
    (A) la proximité de Paris de la résidence
    (B) les heures d'ouverture du bureau de vente
    (C) l'adresse exacte de la résidence
    (D) l'existence d'un appartement modèle

GO ON TO THE NEXT PAGE

En mars 1973, un journal parisien a demandé à des jeunes de 14–15 ans quel était, pour eux, le plus mauvais moment de la journée; plus de la moitié (57%) ont répondu: "Quand je pars le matin pour l'école" et 23% "le temps que je passe à l'école." Tout le monde aussi le sait: beaucoup de lycéens s'ennuient; ils en ont assez, ils en ont "ras le bol." Ce sont des mots qu'on entend et qu'on lit souvent. Certains disent: "Les examens, ça sert à trouver du travail, à avoir un beau métier. Sans diplôme, on ne trouve rien." Mais d'autres pensent que l'école ne sert à rien, qu'ils apprennent plus de choses à la radio, au cinéma, à la télévision ou en voyageant; et aussi que l'école est souvent coupée de la vie et qu'elle est construite, comme la société, avec des chefs, une trop grande hiérarchie.

Ligne (5) ... *(10)*

(*Les Jeunes Aujourd'hui*, Hachette)

73. Ce passage concerne

(A) le nombre d'étudiants dans le système éducatif
(B) les attitudes des adolescents français
(C) le moyen de changer l'attitude des lycéens
(D) des changements récents dans le système éducatif

74. Que veut dire l'expression "ils en ont ras le bol"?

(A) Qu'ils n'ont pas assez à manger
(B) Qu'ils se plaignent des études
(C) Qu'ils doivent se raser
(D) Qu'ils ne veulent plus de quelque chose

75. D'après l'avis de certains étudiants, où est-ce qu'on apprend le plus?

(A) En famille
(B) À l'école
(C) Dans une hiérarchie
(D) Dans la vie

76. Selon les étudiants qui n'aiment pas l'école, quelle est la critique la plus forte contre le système d'éducation courant?

(A) Il y a trop de travail.
(B) Les étudiants s'ennuient.
(C) Les études n'ont rien à voir avec la vie.
(D) Il n'y a pas assez de chefs.

GO ON TO THE NEXT PAGE →

Peu après, le patron m'a fait appeler et, sur le moment, j'ai été ennuyé parce que j'ai pensé qu'il allait me dire de moins téléphoner et de mieux travailler. Ce n'était pas cela *Ligne* du tout. Il m'a déclaré qu'il allait me parler d'un projet (5) encore très vague. Il voulait seulement avoir mon avis sur la question. Il avait l'intention d'installer un bureau à Paris qui traiterait ses affaires sur la place, et directement, avec les grandes compagnies et il voulait savoir si j'étais disposé à y aller. Cela me permettrait de vivre à Paris et aussi de (10) voyager une partie de l'année. "Vous êtes jeune, et il me semble que c'est une vie qui doit vous plaire." J'ai dit que oui mais que dans le fond cela m'était égal.

(Camus, *L'Étranger*, Folio)

77. Le narrateur s'attend à

(A) être grondé par son patron
(B) recevoir une augmentation de salaire
(C) discuter un projet avec le patron
(D) ennuyer le patron

78. Que fait le patron?

(A) Il ennuie le narrateur.
(B) Il lui commande d'aller à Paris.
(C) Il demande ce que pense le narrateur d'une suggestion.
(D) Il refuse de laisser aller le narrateur à Paris.

79. Que veut faire le patron à Paris?

(A) Il veut y habiter.
(B) Il veut travailler pour une grande compagnie.
(C) Il veut ouvrir un bureau.
(D) Il veut trahir sa compagnie.

80. Selon le passage, pour quelle raison le patron a-t-il suggéré le projet au narrateur?

(A) Parce que le narrateur ne travaille pas bien
(B) Parce que le patron pense que le narrateur serait content de cette vie
(C) Parce que le patron est trop jeune pour le faire lui-même
(D) Parce que tout est égal au narrateur

81. Quelle est la réaction du narrateur à l'idée d'aller à Paris?

(A) Il est énervé.
(B) Il est content.
(C) Il se sent rajeuni.
(D) Il ne s'y intéresse pas beaucoup.

GO ON TO THE NEXT PAGE

Quand une rivière est bouchée par une grosse pierre, elle attend, grossit, grossit encore. Et tout à coup la pierre saute, et l'eau, enfin libre, peut continuer son chemin. Il se passe
Ligne souvent la même chose dans l'histoire des arts. Charles
(5) Trenet a fait sauter ce qui bouchait la chanson française, il a fait d'elle un art mais lui a donné, en même temps, une très grande liberté, liberté dans la musique, dans les paroles, et aussi dans les gestes du chanteur sur la scène. Après Trenet, il n'y a plus une chanson, il y a dix, vingt, cent chansons:
(10) après lui les artistes se sentent plus libres de faire, d'écrire, de chanter, ce qu'ils veulent.

(*La Chanson Française Aujourd'hui*, Hachette)

82. Selon le passage, qu'est-ce qui rend une rivière plus grosse?
   (A) L'augmentation de l'eau qui sort de la bouche de la rivière
   (B) La présence de quelque chose qui bloque le chemin
   (C) La présence de pierres
   (D) La liberté de l'eau

83. Pourquoi l'auteur décrit-il une rivière?
   (A) Pour caractériser la musique de Trenet
   (B) Pour expliquer la nature
   (C) Pour montrer l'importance de Trenet
   (D) Pour faire une analogie avec le développement de la chanson

84. D'après ce passage, on comprend qu'avant Trenet la chanson
   (A) était plus comme une rivière
   (B) était plus compliquée
   (C) avait moins de possibilités
   (D) était plus artistique

85. On comprend que Trenet
   (A) a introduit une nouvelle façon de présenter une chanson
   (B) aimait beaucoup la nature
   (C) a écrit cent chansons
   (D) n'était pas aimé par les autres chanteurs

S T O P
IF YOU FINISH BEFORE TIME IS CALLED, YOU MAY CHECK YOUR WORK ON THIS TEST ONLY.
DO NOT WORK ON ANY OTHER TEST IN THIS BOOK.

HOW TO SCORE THE PRINCETON REVIEW
FRENCH SUBJECT TEST

When you take the real exam, the proctors will collect your test booklet and bubble sheet and send your answer sheet to New Jersey where a computer looks at the pattern of filled-in ovals on your answer sheet and gives you a score. We are providing you, however, with this more primitive way of scoring your exam.

DETERMINING YOUR SCORE

STEP 1   Using the answers on the next page, determine how many questions you got right and how many you got wrong on the test. Remember, questions that you do not answer do not count as either right answers or wrong answers.

STEP 2   Write the number of correct answers on line A.

(A) ___80___

STEP 3   Write the number of wrong answers on line B. Divide that number by 3.

(B) ___5___ ÷ 3 = ___1.66___

STEP 4   Subtract the number of wrong answers divided by 3 on line B from the number of correct answers on line A, and round to the nearest whole number. (C) is your **raw score.**

(A) _____ – (B) _____ = (C) 78.33

STEP 5   To determine your **real score,** look up your raw score in the left column of the Score Conversion Table on page 145; the corresponding score on the right is the score you made on the exam.

ANSWERS TO FRENCH SUBJECT TEST 1

Question number	Correct answer	Right	Wrong
1.	C	_____	_____
2.	D	_____	_____
3.	C	_____	_____
4.	D	_____	_____
5.	D	_____	_____
6.	D	_____	_____
7.	B	_____	_____
8.	C	_____	_____
9.	A	_____	_____
10.	D	_____	_____
11.	B	_____	_____
12.	B	_____	_____
13.	A	_____	_____
14.	A	_____	_____
15.	C	_____	_____
16.	A	_____	_____
17.	C	_____	_____
18.	A	_____	_____
19.	A	_____	_____
20.	A	_____	_____
21.	C	_____	_____
22.	B	_____	_____
23.	C	_____	_____
24.	D	_____	_____
25.	C	_____	_____
26.	D	_____	_____
27.	C	_____	_____
28.	B	_____	_____
29.	A	_____	_____
30.	C	_____	_____
31.	C	_____	_____
32.	C	_____	_____
33.	C	_____	_____
34.	A	_____	_____
35.	A	_____	_____

Question number	Correct answer	Right	Wrong
36.	C	_____	_____
37.	B	_____	_____
38.	D	_____	_____
39.	D	_____	_____
40.	D	_____	_____
41.	A	_____	_____
42.	B	_____	_____
43.	A	_____	_____
44.	C	_____	_____
45.	A	_____	_____
46.	C	_____	_____
47.	C	_____	_____
48.	A	_____	_____
49.	D	_____	_____
50.	C	_____	_____
51.	D	_____	_____
52.	A	_____	_____
53.	B	_____	_____
54.	C	_____	_____
55.	D	_____	_____
56.	A	_____	_____
57.	D	_____	_____
58.	A	_____	_____
59.	B	_____	_____
60.	D	_____	_____
61.	D	_____	_____
62.	C	_____	_____
63.	D	_____	_____
64.	C	_____	_____
65.	A	_____	_____
66.	B	_____	_____
67.	D	_____	_____
68.	C	_____	_____
69.	D	_____	_____
70.	C	_____	_____

Question number	Correct answer	Right	Wrong
71.	A	_____	_____
72.	C	_____	_____
73.	B	_____	_____
74.	D	_____	_____
75.	D	_____	_____
76.	C	_____	_____
77.	A	_____	_____
78.	C	_____	_____
79.	C	_____	_____
80.	B	_____	_____
81.	D	_____	_____
82.	B	_____	_____
83.	D	_____	_____
84.	C	_____	_____
85.	A	_____	_____

THE PRINCETON REVIEW FRENCH SUBJECT TEST
SCORE CONVERSION TABLE

Raw score	Scaled score	Raw score	Scaled score	Raw score	Scaled score
85	800	45	630	5	410
84	800	44	620	4	410
83	800	43	620	3	400
82	800	42	610	2	400
81	800	41	610	1	390
80	800	40	600	0	390
79	800	39	600	−1	380
78	800	38	590	−2	380
77	800	37	580	−3	370
76	790	36	580	−4	360
75	790	35	570	−5	360
74	780	34	570	−6	350
73	780	33	560	−7	350
72	770	32	560	−8	340
71	770	31	550	−9	340
70	760	30	550	−10	330
69	760	29	540	−11	330
68	750	28	540	−12	320
67	740	27	530	−13	320
66	740	26	530	−14	310
65	730	25	520	−15	300
64	730	24	520	−16	290
63	720	23	510	−17	290
62	720	22	500	−18	280
61	710	21	500	−19	280
60	710	20	490	−20	270
59	700	19	490	−21	270
58	700	18	480	−22	260
57	690	17	480	−23	260
56	690	16	470	−24	250
55	680	15	470	−25 through −28	240
54	680	14	460		
53	670	13	460		
52	660	12	450		
51	660	11	450		
50	650	10	440		
49	650	9	430		
48	640	8	430		
47	640	7	420		
46	630	6	420		

9

Practice SAT French Subject Test 1: Answers and Explanations

EXPLANATIONS

The possible choices are examined for clues that should have indicated the correct answer. To help explain why a choice is right or wrong, resemblances between English and French words are noted, grammatical explanations are given, and an analysis of the comprehension questions is provided. Key words in the English translations of the questions are in **bold face**, as are the correct answers.

Part A

1. I need to do (pack) my . . . before **leaving on vacation** tomorrow.

   key phrase: *partir en vacances*
   fill in: suitcase

   (A) mouth
   (B) car
   (C) suitcase
   (D) mistake—*faute*, like English "fault"

2. It's **nice outside**; do you want . . . after dinner?

   key phrase: *Il fait beau*
   fill in: to walk, to go outside

   notice that these verbs, used with *te*, are reflexive.

   (A) to wash yourself
   (B) to wonder, to ask yourself
   (C) to get up—*lever*, like English "levitate"
   (D) to go for a walk—*promener*, like English "promenade"

3. The **soldier** waited impatiently for the end of . . .

   key word: *soldat*
   fill in: the war

   (A) the road—*route*, like English "route"
   (B) the train station—look-alike trap: *guerre, gare*
   (C) the war
   (D) the building

4. It is forbidden to keep your shoes **indoors**; leave them . . .

   key phrase: *dans la maison*
   fill in: outside

   (A) moreover
   (B) in agreement
   (C) usually
   (D) outside

5. Paul needs . . . **to hold up his pants.**

key phrase: *soutenir son pantalon*
fill in: a belt, suspenders

(A) an arm
(B) a pocket
(C) a leg
(D) a belt

6. For his **birthday**, the boy received many . . .

key word: *anniversaire*
fill in: presents

(A) days
(B) talents— *talents*, like English
(C) gardens
(D) presents

7. I bought . . . **in the bakery** next door.

key word: *boulangerie*
fill in: bread

(A) fruit—*fruit*, like English
(B) bread
(C) meat
(D) work—*boulot*, familiar for *travail*

8. The . . . of my building is **564**.

key word: 564
fill in: number

(A) number—knee-jerk response: *nombre* is used for
quantity
(B) guide
**(C) numeral—number in the sense of numeral, as
in number "564"**
(D) name—look-alike trap

9. There are **twelve . . . in a year**.

key words: *douze, an*
fill in: months

(A) months
(B) days
(C) hours—*heures*, like English
(D) seasons—*saisons*, like English

10. The movie theater is **empty**; we can . . . anywhere.

key word: *vide*
fill in: sit

(A) to fall asleep
(B) articulate—*articuler*, like English
(C) help ourselves—*assister*, like English "assist"
(D) sit

11. When I wear my favorite **shoes**, I never have sore . . .

key word: *souliers*
fill in: feet

(A) elbows
(B) feet
(C) lips
(D) ears

12. **I agree** with him; I think that he is . . .

key phrase: *d'accord*
fill in: right

(A) wrong
(B) right
(C) hurt
(D) need—*nécessité,* like English "necessity"

13. My office is **located** in a different . . . from my apartment.

key phrase: *se trouve*
fill in: neighborhood, city, area

(A) neighborhood
(B) lawn
(C) trip
(D) plan

14. The **hero** . . . a girl who was in the process of drowning.

key word: *héros*
fill in: saved, rescued

(A) saved
(B) swam—knee-jerk response: you saw *noyer* but not *héros*
(C) thanked
(D) dragged

15. In summer, one should wear . . . **to protect one's eyes**.

    key word: *yeux*
    fill in: glasses (sun)

    (A) shows—*spectacles* looks like "spectacles," see
        page 50
    (B) hair
    (C) glasses
    (D) rays—you saw *soleil*, but not *protéger*

16. One must pay attention before . . . **the road.**

    key words: *la rue*
    fill in: crossing

    (A) to cross—*traverser*, like English "traverse"
    (B) to sweat
    (C) to translate
    (D) to transform—*transformer*, like English

17. It is **not nice** . . . your friends.

    key phrase: *ce n'est pas gentil*
    fill in: to be mean to, to hurt, to tease

    (A) to read
    (B) to fill
    (C) to tease
    (D) to tolerate—*tolérer*, like English

18. The constant **noise** . . .

    key word: *bruit*
    fill in: annoys me, upsets me

    (A) annoys me
    (B) teaches me
    (C) lifts me up
    (D) shuts me in

19. The **waiter** . . . my glass of wine.

    key word: *serveur*
    fill in: filled, spilled, brought

    (A) filled
    (B) pushed back
    (C) climbed (again)
    (D) saw (again)

20. The lady . . . her **arm to catch the ball.**

key words: *bras, attraper*
fill in: extended, reached out

(A) extended
(B) overturned, spilled
(C) withdrew—*retiré*, like English "retire"
(D) lost

21. The student **wrote** . . . on the work of Maupassant.

key word: *écrit*
fill in: an essay, a paper

(A) a pellet
(B) a recipe
(C) a dissertation, a paper
(D) a witness

22. Without the protection of an umbrella, I will be . . . by the **rain.**

key word: *pluie*
fill in: soaked

(A) tempted—look-alike for *trempé*
(B) soaked
(C) stretched, strained
(D) tempered—*tempéré*, like English

23. The trains **run less often** on . . . days.

key phrase: *passent moins souvent*
fill in: holidays

(A) normal—*normaux*, like English
(B) free
(C) holidays
(D) currents—*courants*, like English

24. The **mountain climbers** are going to . . . **a climb** of Mount Kilimanjaro.

key words: *alpinistes, ascension*
fill in: attempt, try

(A) modify
(B) show—misleading look-alike (*montrer* resembles *monter*, to climb)
(C) pull
(D) attempt

25. **Years of use** will . . . **the leather** of these boots.

key words: *années d'usage, cuir*
fill in: break in, wear out, soften

(A) besiege
(B) reduce—*réduire*, like English
(C) soften—from *souple*, "supple"
(D) surprise

26. If I leave now, I can . . . **rush hour.**

key phrase: *l'heure d'affluence*
fill in: avoid, miss

(A) estimate—*estimer*, like English
(B) see again
(C) arrange—*arranger*, like English
(D) avoid

Part B

27. Pronouns

(A) no negative to go with *ne*
(B) no pronoun to indicate what is being suggested
(C) correct: *ne* plus a negative
(D) *rien* must be used with *ne*

28. Pronouns

(A) *que* is never used with a preposition
(B) correct: *qui* can be used with prepositions
(C) which—makes no sense
(D) what—makes no sense

29. Odds and Ends: Articles

**(A) correct: *homme* is masculine but because it
    starts with a silent "h" it takes *cet* and not *ce***
(B) *huile* would require *cette*
(C) *dame* would require the feminine *cette*
(D) *livre* would require the regular masculine *ce*

30. Pronouns

The required pronoun needs to refer to place or
location.
(A) *en* will only refer to location if used with a verb
    that normally takes *de* (*Vient-il de là-bas? Oui, il
    en vient.*)
(B) *où* meaning "where" is used like *qui* or *que* to
    connect phrases
(C) correct: *y* refers to place
(D) *là* means "there"

31. Prepositions

    (A) the correct expression would be *au Mexique*
    (B) the correct expression would be *en France*
    (C) correct: for cities, you use *à*
    (D) the correct expression would be *en Chine*

32. Odds and Ends: Adjective vs. Adverb

    (A) adjective—cannot modify a verb
    (B) *jamais* requires *ne*
    (C) correct: adverb—can modify a verb
    (D) adjective—cannot modify a verb

33. Pronouns

    (A) subject pronoun
    (B) indirect object pronoun
    (C) correct: stressed pronoun as the object of a preposition
    (D) reflexive pronoun

34. Prepositions

    (A) correct: *réfléchir* requires *à*
    (B) you cannot say *réfléchir sans*
    (C) you cannot say *réfléchir avec*
    (D) you cannot use *dont* with *laquelle*

35. Verbs

    (A) correct: *vendre* requires *avoir*—"has sold"
    (B) *être* would form a passive tense, "is sold"—does not work
    (C) no need for subjunctive
    (D) *vendre* requires *avoir*, and there is no need for subjunctive

36. Prepositions

    (A) *s'excuser* is reflexive and cannot be used with another object
    (B) *résister* must be used with *à*
    (C) correct: *considérer* takes a direct object
    (D) *réfléchir* must be used with *à*

37. Verbs

    (A) the present doesn't work here since the other action is in the past
    (B) correct: imperfect—he was outside in an ongoing way in the past
    (C) no need for subjunctive or present
    (D) no need for conditional

38. Verbs

    (A) imperfect—cannot follow an imperfect clause beginning with *si*

    (B) no need for the past conditional

    (C) the future

    (D) correct: if the *si* clause uses the imperfect, the following clause will use the present conditional

39. Pronouns

    (A) in this context, *laver* needs to be reflexive

    (B) *brosser* is used for teeth, not hands

    (C) *serrer la main*, to shake hands

    (D) correct: the expression is *se laver les mains*

40. Prepositions

    (A) *décider* takes *de*

    (B) *avoir le droit* takes *de*

    (C) *avoir envie* takes *de*

    (D) correct: *vouloir* takes a direct object

41. Verbs

    (A) correct: *il faut que* requires the subjunctive

    (B) present indicative

    (C) future—wrong tense

    (D) imperfect—wrong tense

42. Pronouns

    (A) subject pronoun

    (B) correct: stressed pronoun as the object of the preposition

    (C) reflexive pronoun

    (D) indirect object pronoun

43. Verbs

    (A) correct: present

    (B) no need for subjunctive, nothing is hypothetical

    (C) imperfect cannot be used since action has not taken place yet

    (D) the future is possible but requires *ce—ce sera*

44. Odds and Ends

    (A) *si difficile* is not a comparative

    (B) *le meilleur* is a superlative, not a comparative

    (C) correct: *pire* can be used to compare two things

    (D) *trop* is an adverb that needs to modify a verb, an adjective, or another adverb

45. Prepositions

    (A) correct: *durant* means "during"
    (B) *sinon* means "otherwise"
    (C) *afin de* means "in order to"
    (D) *avant que* must be followed by a clause with a verb

46. Pronouns

    (A) this leaves the sentence incomplete
    (B) *tu* would take the verb form *as—tu m'as écrit*
    (C) correct: "it is he who"
    (D) *personne* requires *ne* in a sentence

Part C

47. Verbs

    (A) imperfect indicates an ongoing action in the past
    (B) conditional indicates one thing happening because of another
    (C) correct: present
    (D) past imperfect indicates an ongoing action that was completed in the past

48. Verbs

    (A) correct: no agreement
    (B) no need for feminine
    (C) no need for plural
    (D) no need for feminine plural

49. Vocabulary

    (A) past—makes no sense
    (B) unpleasant (i.e., bad weather)—makes no sense
    (C) sad—makes no sense
    (D) correct: *favorable* (i.e., good weather)

50. Vocabulary

    (A) far from
    (B) never
    (C) correct: finally
    (D) simply

51. Prepositions

    (A) you cannot say partir *dans* Tokyo
    (B) without—makes no sense
    (C) you cannot say *partir en* Tokyo
    (D) correct: *partir pour Tokyo*

52. Vocabulary

    (A) correct: to attend
    (B) to knock down
    (C) to sit
    (D) to aspire, to inhale, etc.

53. Vocabulary

    (A) in spite (of the fact)
    (B) correct: because—*parce que*
    (C) without
    (D) as soon as

54. Vocabulary

    key words: *mais, les dangers*

    (A) proud
    (B) annoyed
    (C) correct: calm
    (D) heavy

55. Vocabulary

    key words: *avion, piste*

    (A) to get rid of
    (B) to overflow
    (C) to develop
    (D) correct: to take off

56. Odds and Ends: Adjectives

    (A) correct: past participle or adjective
    (B) verb: to study
    (C) noun: a study
    (D) noun: a student

57. Vocabulary

    key word: *longuement*

    (A) minutes
    (B) seconds
    (C) moments
    (D) correct: weeks

58. Verbs

    (A) correct: present—follows *Maintenant*
    (B) imperfect
    (C) conditional
    (D) *passé composé*

Part D

59. What did the couple do before looking for the café?

    (A) "They waited."
    **(B) "They took their car to a garage.": correct—
    another way of saying *Ayant laissé la voiture au
    garage...***
    (C) "They spoke to two children.": familiar words—
    wrong context
    (D) "They hit something.": familiar words—wrong
    context

60. Where is the couple?

(A) *À Chartres*: familiar words—wrong context
(B) "in a village": *ne formaient pas un village*
(C) "in a big town": common sense—if it's not even a village, it's certainly not a city
(D) "in a suburb of the town": correct—key words are *un faubourg lointain*

61. For what reason did the couple go to the café?

(A) "to eat a good meal": no, since *Ils commandèrent n'importe quoi pour justifier leur présence.*
(B) "to find someone to talk to": no context for this
(C) "to ask directions": no context for this
(D) "to pass the time": correct—*ils décidèrent d'attendre dans un café.*

62. What does the author mean by *"l'heure creuse"*?

(A) "that there were a lot of people in the café": incorrect—the café was empty
(B) "that it was almost night": no context for this
(C) "that no one was there": correct—*Il n'y avait personne.*
(D) "that it was time for the café to close": no context for this

63. What impression did the lady have at the café?

(A) "that she had eaten cotton": familiar words— wrong context
(B) "that she had on too much makeup": familiar words—wrong context
(C) "that there was too much noise": familiar words—wrong context
(D) "that she couldn't hear": correct—*les bruits ne lui parvenaient qu'assourdis.*

_____

64. The author writes in a style that is

(A) "serious"
(B) "neutral": the author is obviously doing more than just describing the scene
(C) "humorous": correct—tip-offs are word play (*rangé, se range*), exaggeration
(D) "scientific"

65. What makes the race car driver appear?

(A) "the act of getting behind the wheel": *et que réveille le simple contact du pied sur l'accélérateur.*
(B) "the sunrise"
(C) "the action of waking up"
(D) "a horn": familiar word—*klaxonner*—but wrong context

66. According to the passage, Jérôme Charnelet is usually

(A) "a race car driver": familiar words—wrong context

(B) "of an amiable disposition": correct—*ce bon père de famille* . . .

(C) "impatient"

(D) "generous"

67. How does Jérôme react to the green light?

(A) "He stops.": makes no sense

(B) "He swats a fly.": familiar words—wrong context

(C) "He has trouble seeing colors.": you're interpreting too literally

(D) "He becomes a crazy driver.": correct—*il voit rouge*

68. What would convince Jérôme to change his position on the road?

(A) "the realization that he is in the middle of the road": familiar words—wrong context

(B) "his sense of obligation to the other drivers": familiar words—wrong context

(C) "the horns of other drivers": correct—*après avoir subi une klaxonnade nourrie. . .*"After having been subjected to continuous honking. . ."

(D) "the color of the traffic light": familiar words—wrong context

69. We understand that Jérôme drives in a manner that is

(A) "orderly"

(B) "steady": familiar word—*rangée*—but wrong context

(C) "gracious"

(D) "obsessed": correct—*obsédée*; the key word is *démoniaque*

---

70. These apartments

(A) "will be renovated in 2005"—no context for this

(B) "were renovated in the 19th century"—familiar words—wrong context

(C) "are being renovated": correct—"*en cours de rénovation*"

(D) "are renovated"

71. This publicity is aimed at

(A) "prospective buyers": correct—"*bureau de vente*"

(B) "future tenants"—no context for this

(C) "elderly people"—no context for this

(D) "sellers"—familiar word—wrong context

72. After reading this publicity one is aware of everything BUT of

(A) "the proximity of Paris to the residence"—*aux portes de Paris*

(B) "the opening hours of the sales office"—*du lundi au samedi de 9 h 30 à 19 h*

(C) "the precise address of the residence": correct— this is the only thing one does not know about these apartments

(D) "the existence of a show apartment"— *appartement-témoin*

_____

73. This passage is concerned with

(A) "the number of students in the educational system": incorrect—percentages are given, not numbers

(B) "the attitudes of French adolescents": correct

(C) "the way to change the attitude of French students": no context for this

(D) "recent changes in the educational system": no context for this

74. What does the expression *"ils en ont ras le bol"* mean?

(A) "that they does not have enough to eat"

(B) "that they complain about their studies"

(C) "that they should shave"

(D) "that they are sick and tired of something": correct—*ils en ont assez*

75. According to certain students, where does one learn the most?

(A) "at home": no context for this

(B) "at school": obviously incorrect

(C) "in a hierarchy": incorrect—this is one of the problems

(D) "in life": correct—*à la radio, au cinéma, à la télévision ou en voyageant...*

76. What is the strongest criticism of the educational system?

(A) "There is too much work.": no context for this

(B) "The students are bored.": a concern, but not the biggest problem

(C) correct: *l'école est souvent coupée de la vie...* "school is often cut off from life..."

(D) "There are not enough bosses.": just the opposite

_____

77. The narrator expects

   (A) "to be scolded by his boss": correct—*j'ai pensé qu'il allait me dire de moins téléphoner et de mieux travailler.*

   (B) "to get a raise": no context for this

   (C) "to discuss a project with his boss": no context for this

   (D) "to annoy the boss": familiar words—wrong context

78. What does the boss do?

   (A) "He annoys the narrator.": familiar words—wrong context

   (B) "He orders him to go to Paris.": too strong—the boss asks if he wants to go

   (C) "He asks what the narrator thinks of a question.": correct—*il voulait seulement avoir mon avis sur la question.*

   (D) "He refuses to let the narrator go to Paris.": wrong

79. What does the boss want to do in Paris?

   (A) "He wants to live there.": perhaps, but too vague to be a good answer

   (B) "He wants to work for a big company.": familiar words—wrong context

   (C) "He wants to open an office.": correct—*l'intention d'installer un bureau à Paris. . .*

   (D) "He wishes to betray his company.": no evidence for this

80. Why does the boss suggest the project to the narrator?

   (A) "because the narrator isn't working well": no, the narrator is evidently being rewarded

   (B) "because he thinks the narrator would be happy with such a life": correct—*il me semble que c'est une vie qui doit vous plaire.*

   (C) "because the boss is too young to do it himself": familiar words—but misleading

   (D) "because it's all the same to the narrator": familiar words—wrong context

81. What reaction does the narrator have to the idea of going to Paris?

   (A) "He is irritated.": no context for this

   (B) "He is happy.": he is neither happy nor unhappy

   (C) "He feels rejuvenated.": no context for this

   (D) "He's not very interested.": correct—*dans le fond cela m'était égal.*

82. What makes a river bigger?

   (A) "an increase in water that comes from the mouth of the river": familiar words—wrong context
   (B) "the presence of something that blocks the way": correct—*Quand une rivière est bouchée par une grosse pierre...*
   (C) "the presence of rocks": familiar words—wrong context
   (D) "the freedom of water": familiar words—wrong context

83. Why does the author describe a river?

   (A) "to characterize Trenet's music": not in this case
   (B) "to explain nature": makes no sense
   (C) "to show Trenet's importance": tricky—but not an answer to this question
   (D) "to make an analogy to the development of song": correct—*il se passe souvent la même chose dans l'histoire des arts.*

84. It is inferred that before Trenet, the song (in this context, *la chanson* means songs in general)

   (A) "was more like a river": makes no sense
   (B) "was more complicated": no context for this
   (C) "had fewer possibilities": correct—*après lui les artistes se sentent plus libres...*
   (D) "was more artistic": no context for this

85. One can infer that Trenet

   (A) "introduced a new way of presenting a song": correct—*Charles Trenet a fait sauter ce qui bouchait la chanson française...*
   (B) "loved nature": makes no sense
   (C) "wrote a hundred songs": familiar words but wrong contex
   (D) "wasn't liked by other singers": no context for this

10

Practice SAT French Subject Test 2

FRENCH SUBJECT TEST 2

SECTION 2

Your responses to the SAT French questions must be filled in on Section 2 of your answer sheet (at the back of the book). Marks on any other section will not be counted toward your score.

When your supervisor gives the signal, turn the page and begin the SAT French Subject Test. There are 100 numbered ovals on the answer sheet and 85 questions in the SAT French Subject Test. Therefore, use only ovals 1 to 85 for recording your answers.

FRENCH SUBJECT TEST 2

PLEASE NOTE THAT YOUR ANSWER SHEET HAS FIVE ANSWER POSITIONS MARKED A, B, C, D, E, WHILE THE QUESTIONS THROUGHOUT THIS TEST CONTAIN ONLY FOUR CHOICES. BE SURE <u>NOT</u> TO MAKE ANY MARKS IN COLUMN E.

Part A

<u>Directions:</u> This part consists of a number of incomplete statements, each having four suggested completions. Select the most appropriate completion and fill in the corresponding oval on the answer sheet.

---

1. Il est encore . . . . On va rater le train.

   (A) en avance
   (B) à l'heure
   (C) en retard
   (D) d'accord

2. N'oublie pas ton parapluie, il va . . . ce soir.

   (A) pleurer
   (B) faire froid
   (C) ouvrir
   (D) pleuvoir

3. Il n'y a plus rien dans le réfrigérateur. Il faut que j'aille . . .

   (A) prendre une douche
   (B) tondre le gazon
   (C) faire les courses
   (D) mettre le couvert

4. J'ai mal au . . . . Je vais prendre rendez-vous chez l'orthopédiste.

   (A) nez
   (B) genou
   (C) oreilles
   (D) médecin

5. Sa voiture est toujours en panne et il en a vraiment . . .

   (A) marre
   (B) mer
   (C) miel
   (D) dégoûté

6. Au crépuscule, le ciel . . . de mille feux.

   (A) éteignait
   (B) disparaissait
   (C) tombait
   (D) brillait

7. Il a trouvé très difficile l'examen qu'il a . . . hier.

   (A) passé
   (B) pris
   (C) attrapé
   (D) reçu

8. Jean va acheter des livres à la . . .

   (A) boucherie
   (B) librairie
   (C) pâtisserie
   (D) bibliothèque

9. Elle est si allergique à la poussière qu'elle . . . sans arrêt.

   (A) éclate
   (B) éclabousse
   (C) éternue
   (D) embrasse

10. Il a tout fait pour atteindre son . . .

   (A) test
   (B) travail
   (C) branche
   (D) but

GO ON TO THE NEXT PAGE ➡

11. Il s'est évanoui en apprenant . . .

    (A) la nouvelle
    (B) la leçon
    (C) le fauteuil
    (D) la poubelle

12. Personne ne répond à la porte; elle n'est probablement pas . . .

    (A) là
    (B) dessus
    (C) dessous
    (D) à côté

13. La voiture . . . net devant l'enfant qui traversait la rue en courant.

    (A) s'emporta
    (B) s'assura
    (C) s'arrêta
    (D) s'écria

14. Ils ont choisi d'habiter . . . avec leurs trois petits enfants.

    (A) en banlieue
    (B) en chemin
    (C) en cachette
    (D) en retard

15. Ils sont pleins d'énergie et sont . . . tous les matins à 6 heures.

    (A) étendus
    (B) assis
    (C) debout
    (D) fâchés

16. Ne sachant que faire, j'ai demandé . . . à mon avocat.

    (A) conseil
    (B) contribution
    (C) contact
    (D) compagnie

17. Pour son entrevue avec son futur employeur demain, elle va mettre . . .

    (A) un soulier
    (B) un tailleur
    (C) un costume
    (D) un portemanteau

18. Elle a . . . beaucoup d'argent pour acheter sa maison.

    (A) prêté
    (B) renversé
    (C) emprunté
    (D) vendu

19. Pour faire ce gâteau, vous . . . de beaucoup de sucre.

    (A) avez envie
    (B) avez besoin
    (C) avez soif
    (D) avez peur

20. Il est exténué; il a . . . travaillé.

    (A) peu
    (B) bientôt
    (C) souvent
    (D) trop

GO ON TO THE NEXT PAGE

Part B

Directions: Each of the following sentences contains a blank. From the four choices given, select the one that can be inserted in the blank to form a grammatically correct sentence and fill in the corresponding oval on the answer sheet. Choice (A) may consist of dashes that indicate that no insertion is required to form a grammatically correct sentence.

21. Le livre ------- j'ai perdu hier est à mon frère.

    (A) dont
    (B) à qui
    (C) que
    (D) lequel

22. Je suis passée à la maison ------- prendre mon parapluie.

    (A) à
    (B) pour
    (C) parce que
    (D) après

23. Mon père revenait toujours ------- à la maison entre midi et deux heures.

    (A) déjeuner
    (B) déjeuné
    (C) déjeunait
    (D) déjeunant

24. Elle est rentrée ------- Danemark hier soir.

    (A) de
    (B) du
    (C) en
    (D) aux

25. Elle dessine beaucoup ------- que son frère.

    (A) bien
    (B) meilleur
    (C) mal
    (D) mieux

26. La robe qu'elle a ------- hier n'est vraiment pas à la mode.

    (A) mise
    (B) acheté
    (C) mis
    (D) enfiler

27. Il ne sera pas là demain ------- il vient de partir en voyage d'affaires.

    (A) bien qu'
    (B) avant qu'
    (C) puisqu'
    (D) à moins qu'

28. Regarde ------- tu mets les pieds quand tu marches.

    (A) là
    (B) où
    (C) vers
    (D) près de

GO ON TO THE NEXT PAGE

29. Appelle-moi ------- prendre une décision.

    (A) en
    (B) pendant
    (C) avant de
    (D) à

30. Bien que ------- débordée de travail, j'essaierai de passer te voir ce soir.

    (A) j'étais
    (B) je serais
    (C) je sois
    (D) je suis

31. Est-ce que tu veux un bonbon? Oui, j'en veux bien -------.

    (A) quelque
    (B) peu
    (C) un peu
    (D) un

32. Est-ce que Marie est déjà partie à la poste? Non, mais elle va ------- aller tout de suite.

    (A) y
    (B) en
    (C) toujours
    (D) demain

33. Si elle s'entraînait plus sérieusement, elle ------- toutes les courses.

    (A) gagnerait
    (B) gagnait
    (C) gagnera
    (D) a gagné

34. Il faut que ------- à la banque demain matin pour retirer de l'argent.

    (A) j'allais
    (B) j'aille
    (C) j'irai
    (D) j'irais

GO ON TO THE NEXT PAGE

Part C

<u>Directions</u>: The paragraphs below contain blank spaces indicating omissions in the text. For some blanks it is necessary to choose the completion that is most appropriate to the meaning of the passage; for other blanks, to choose the one completion that forms a grammatically correct sentence. In some instances, choice (A) may consist of dashes that indicate that no insertion is required to form a grammatically correct sentence. In each case, indicate your answer by filling in the corresponding oval on the answer sheet. Be sure to read the paragraph completely before answering the questions related to it.

Il n'avait pas mangé ------- le matin. Les cafés qu'il rencontrait à ------- pas l'intimidaient et

35. (A) après
    (B) depuis
    (C) pour
    (D) dans

36. (A) tous
    (B) chacun
    (C) chaque
    (D) quelque

------- dégoûtaient, à cause de la foule qui ------- était ------- . Il s'adressa ------- un gendarme.

37. (A) lui
    (B) la
    (C) le
    (D) leur

38. (A) en
    (B) y
    (C) dans
    (D) où

39. (A) entassé
    (B) entasser
    (C) entassées
    (D) entassée

40. (A) à
    (B) vers
    (C) avec
    (D) pour

Mais il était si lent à ------- ses mots que l'autre ne se donna même pas la peine de l'écouter -------

41. (A) trouvé
    (B) trouver
    (C) trouvés
    (D) trouvait

42. (A) à travers
    (B) jusque-là
    (C) au
    (D) jusqu'au

bout et lui tourna ------- , au milieu de la phrase, en ------- les épaules. Il continua machinalement

43. (A) la tête
    (B) le dos
    (C) l'oreille
    (D) les yeux

44. (A) tirant
    (B) portant
    (C) haussant
    (D) passant

------- marcher.

45. (A) -------
    (B) pour
    (C) à
    (D) en

GO ON TO THE NEXT PAGE

Cher Monsieur, La lettre ------- je vous ------- adressée le 1er juillet ------- restée sans réponse, je me

46. (A) -------
    (B) laquelle
    (C) dont
    (D) que

47. (A) aie
    (B) ai
    (C) aurai
    (D) avait

48. (A) ayant
    (B) avant
    (C) étant
    (D) était

permets de vous écire pour ------- prier de prendre ma requête ------- considération.

49. (A) te
    (B) me
    (C) vous
    (D) le

50. (A) en
    (B) avec
    (C) par
    (D) comme

Quand j'étais petit, mes parents ------- emmenaient ------- nager à la piscine municipale de

51. (A) leur
    (B) te
    (C) s'
    (D) m'

52. (A) peut-être
    (B) pourtant
    (C) une fois
    (D) souvent

Roubaix. Un de mes amis d'enfance ------- de m'apprendre ------- cette piscine a été -------

53. (A) vient
    (B) est venu
    (C) viendra
    (D) viennent

54. (A) qui
    (B) que
    (C) puisque
    (D) dès que

55. (A) démolie
    (B) construite
    (C) transformée
    (D) créée

------- beaucoup d'originalité en un beau musée d'art et d'industrie.

56. (A) sur
    (B) avec
    (C) par
    (D) comme

GO ON TO THE NEXT PAGE

Part D

<u>Directions</u>: Read the following texts carefully for comprehension. Each is followed by a number of questions or incomplete statements. Select the completion or answer that is best according to the text and fill in the corresponding oval on the answer sheet.

"L'été est trop long," disait la grand-mère qui accueillait du même soupir soulagé la pluie d'automne et le départ de Jacques, dont les piétinements d'ennui au
Ligne long des journées torrides, dans les pièces aux persiennes
(5) closes, ajoutaient encore à son énervement.
    Elle ne comprenait pas d'ailleurs qu'une période de l'année fût plus spécialement désignée pour n'y rien faire. "Je n'ai jamais eu de vacances, moi," disait-elle, et c'était vrai, elle n'avait connu ni l'école ni le loisir, elle avait
(10) travaillé enfant, et travaillé sans relâche. Elle admettait que, pour un bénéfice plus grand, son petit-fils pendant quelques années ne rapporte pas d'argent à la maison. Mais, dès le premier jour, elle avait commencé de ruminer sur ces trois mois perdus, et, lorsque Jacques entra en
(15) troisième, elle jugea qu'il était temps de lui trouver l'emploi de ses vacances. "Tu vas travailler cet été," lui dit-elle à la fin de l'année scolaire," et rapporter un peu d'argent à la maison. Tu ne peux pas rester comme ça sans rien faire."

(Albert Camus, *Le premier homme*, Folio)

57. Quand arrivait la pluie d'automne, la grand-mère était

  (A) énervée
  (B) triste
  (C) contente
  (D) fière

58. Pendant les mois d'été, Jacques

  (A) travaillait beaucoup
  (B) passait son temps à lire
  (C) s'amusait sans arrêt
  (D) ne savait comment se distraire

59. Quand elle était petite, la grand-mère

  (A) avait de moins longues vacances que Jacques
  (B) dessinait pendant ses loisirs
  (C) passait tout son temps au travail
  (D) ne faisait jamais rien

60. D'après le texte, on comprend que

  (A) Jacques poursuit ses études
  (B) la grand-mère ne veut pas que Jacques aille encore à l'école
  (C) la grand-mère refuse que Jacques travaille pendant l'été
  (D) Jacques est le troisième de sa classe

61. La grand-mère veut que Jacques ait un emploi pour qu'il

  (A) ait un peu d'argent de poche
  (B) puisse payer ses études
  (C) contribue aux dépenses de la famille
  (D) apprenne un métier

GO ON TO THE NEXT PAGE →

Avant de venir au Central, lisait-il, je viens d'assister à une scène d'une atroce beauté.

On a trouvé cette nuit près de la Puerta del Sol un
Ligne enfant de trois ans qui pleurait perdu, dans les ténèbres.
(5) Or, une des femmes réfugiées dans les sous-sols de la Gran Via ignorait ce qu'était devenu son enfant, un petit garçon du même âge, blond comme l'enfant trouvé dans la Puerta del Sol. On lui donne la nouvelle. Elle court à la maison où l'on garde l'enfant, calle Montera. Dans
(10) la demi-obscurité d'une boutique aux rideaux baissés, l'enfant suce un morceau de chocolat. La mère s'avance vers lui, les bras tendus, mais ses yeux s'agrandissent, prennent une fixité terrible, démente.

Ce n'est pas son enfant.
(15) Elle reste immobile de longues minutes. L'enfant perdu lui sourit. Alors elle se précipite sur lui, le serre contre elle, l'emporte en pensant à l'enfant qu'on n'a pas retrouvé.

(André Malraux, *L'espoir*, Folio Plus)

62. L'enfant de trois ans pleure parce qu'
    (A) il a perdu son morceau de chocolat
    (B) il s'est fait mal
    (C) il ne sait pas où est sa famille
    (D) il fait nuit

63. Les rideaux de la boutique sont
    (A) ouverts
    (B) levés
    (C) descendus
    (D) déchirés

64. La femme "se précipite sur lui" veut dire qu'elle va vers l'enfant
    (A) en courant
    (B) à pas lents
    (C) en pleurant
    (D) avec nonchalance

65. Elle "le serre contre elle" signifie qu'elle
    (A) le repousse
    (B) l'embrasse
    (C) lui sourit
    (D) le frappe

66. A qui la femme pense-t-elle en emportant l'enfant ?
    (A) A son propre fils
    (B) Au fils d'une des refugiées
    (C) Au fils du lecteur
    (D) Au fils d'un garde

GO ON TO THE NEXT PAGE

TRAIN + VOITURE: EN TOUTE LIBERTÉ

Evitez les bouchons des grands départs!

En choisissant la formule "Train + Location de voitures," vous êtes sûrs de bénéficier de tous les avantages: le confort du train, la liberté de la voiture … Tout en réalisant de vraies **économies!**

Pratique: à la descente du train, votre voiture vous attend en gare.

Economique: vous bénéficiez d'une réduction importante sur votre location.

Efficace: vous réservez votre voiture en même temps que votre train.

Pour profiter de cette offre:

– Réservez votre place.

– En fin de commande, cliquez sur "AJOUTER UNE VOITURE."

– Choisissez l'offre "Train + Location de Voitures."

67. Les bouchons dont il est question dans le texte

 (A) servent à boucher les bouteilles
 (B) sont des embouteillages
 (C) retardent les trains
 (D) évitent de perdre du temps

68. D'après le texte, la solution Train + Location de Voitures

 (A) revient plus cher
 (B) coûte trop cher
 (C) n'est guère pratique
 (D) est une bonne affaire

GO ON TO THE NEXT PAGE ➤

Les Français auraient-ils attrapé le virus du home cinéma ? A en croire la grande majorité des constructeurs d'électronique grand public, la réponse ne fait pas de
Ligne doute. Les équipements liés au cinéma à domicile, qui
(5) englobent aussi bien de la hi-fi que de la vidéo, ont le vent en poupe. Tous les professionnels du secteur s'accordent même pour dire que 2002 devrait être l'année de l'explosion de ce marché en France. Près de 4 millions de téléviseurs, dont 15% avec un écran au format cinéma
(10) 16/9, devraient ainsi être vendus en 2002 selon les prévisions de l'institut GFK.

"Il y a toujours eu en France une forte sensibilité des gens à consommer des films à la maison," explique Jean-Marc Auffret, responsable marketing home cinéma
(15) chez Sony France. "Mais jusqu' à présent le home cinéma était réservé à une frange très cinéphile et relativement aisée financièrement. Aujourd'hui, avec l'apparition des appareils combinés et la baisse des prix de certains éléments audiovisuels, le grand public peut
(20) plus facilement s'équipper." Il est sans doute encore trop tôt pour parler de démocratisation—installer un ensemble home cinéma coûte toujours entre 1300 et plus de 60000 euros selon les matériels choisis—mais les constructeurs disposent de plus en plus de produits
(25) abordables. Aujourd'hui, il est possible d'acheter un ensemble composé d'un lecteur de DVD équipé d'un amplificateur et d'un pack de six enceintes pour moins de 700 euros.

(Guillaume Fraissard, *Le Monde*, 31 mai, 2002)

69. D'après cet article, les Français

(A) vont de plus en plus souvent au cinéma
(B) vont rarement au cinéma
(C) préfèrent regarder la télévision
(D) aiment de plus en plus regarder des films chez eux

70. Les équipements liés au cinéma à domicile

(A) ont de plus en plus de succès
(B) ne sont pas nouveaux
(C) n'ont guère d'intérêt
(D) ne sont pas dans le vent

71. Aujourd'hui, l'audiovisuel est

(A) plus coûteux
(B) meilleur marché
(C) hors de prix
(D) inabordable

72. "Le grand public" représente

(A) quelques privilégiés
(B) les gens célèbres
(C) les amateurs de cinéma
(D) la plupart des gens

73. " . . . les constructeurs disposent de plus en plus de produits abordables" signifie qu'ils

(A) s'en débarrassent
(B) en ont besoin
(C) y ont accès
(D) en fabriquent

GO ON TO THE NEXT PAGE

Voici la recette des madeleines, ces petits gâteaux de forme ovale au ventre bombé, si chers à Marcel Proust:

La veille, mélangez soigneusement les ingrédients suivants jusqu'à l'obtention d'une pâte parfaitement lisse:

Madeleines

Farine	90 gr
Sucre	90 gr
Levure	2 gr
Miel de Provence	10 gr
Oeufs	2
Beurre fondu	90 gr
Le zeste d'un citron	
Pastis (facultatif)	1 cl

Conservez cette pâte au réfrigérateur.

Le lendemain, distribuez la pâte dans 12 moules à madeleines beurrés. Enfournez à four moyen et laissez cuire jusqu'à ce que les gâteaux aient une belle couleur dorée. Démoulez sur une grille à la sortie du four, laissez refroidir, et dégustez!

74. Quand faut-il préparer la pâte des madeleines?

(A) Le lendemain
(B) Le jour précédent
(C) Deux heures à l'avance
(D) Hier

75. D'après la recette, le pastis est un ingrédient

(A) indispensable
(B) sucré
(C) optionnel
(D) parfumé

GO ON TO THE NEXT PAGE ➡

Le bossu reparut, une brochure à la main. Il s'installa commodément, les coudes sur la table, son menton entre ses mains.

Ligne

(5) "Je vous ai déjà laissé entendre, dit-il, que j'avais des projets d'une assez grande envergure."

"De vastes projets."

"C'est cela même, et je vais vous les révéler aujourd'hui." "Il prit le ton d'un conférencier."

"Ce qui m'a attiré ici, c'est d'abord mon amour de

(10) la nature. Mais quoique je ne manque pas d'argent en ce moment, j'ai une famille à nourrir, et je dois assurer l'avenir de ma fillette: c'est pourquoi le philosophe que je suis a voulu concilier son désir de la vie naturelle et l'obligation où il se trouve de faire fortune."

(15) De ce discours, Ugolin ne retint que les derniers mots. Il avait l'intention de "faire fortune." Faire fortune aux Romarins ! Avec quoi? Sûrement pas avec ces oliviers à demi morts, ni ces amandiers à l'agonie; ni avec des légumes, ni avec du blé, ni avec du vin. Il connaissait

(20) donc la source, et il voulait peut-être planter des oeillets! C'est pourquoi, par une contre-attaque désespérée, il dit: "Vous savez ici, les fleurs, même si vous aviez une belle source. . ."

"Quelles fleurs?" "dit le bossu d'un air surpris." Croyez-vous que j'espère faire fortune en vendant des églantines ou des chardons? Et quelle source? Vous savez que celle que je possède est bien loin d'ici"!

(Marcel Pagnol, *Jean de Florette*, Presses Pocket)

76. "Je vous ai déjà laissé entendre" signifie "je vous ai déjà"

(A) dit
(B) répété
(C) suggéré
(D) menti

77. Le bossu a de "vastes projets" parce qu'il

(A) a besoin d'argent tout de suite
(B) pense à l'avenir de sa fille
(C) est philosophe
(D) aime beaucoup l'argent

78. Du discours du bossu, Ugolin se souvient

(A) uniquement des derniers mots
(B) peut-être des premiers mots
(C) toujours de la dernière phrase
(D) de tout sauf de la fin

79. Aux lignes 19–23, à l'annonce des projets du bossu, Ugolin est

(A) amusé
(B) paniqué, très inquiet
(C) rempli de joie
(D) rassuré

80. Ugolin cherche à savoir si le bossu

(A) va planter des vignes
(B) va sauver les oliviers et les amandiers
(C) compte vendre des chardons
(D) connaît l'existence de la source

GO ON TO THE NEXT PAGE

Vous comprenez tout de suite que la vraie ville est l'arsenal, que l'autre ne vit que par lui, qu'il déborde sur elle. Sous toutes les formes, en tous lieux, à, tous
Ligne les coins réapparaissent l'administration, la discipline,
(5) la feuille de papier rayé, le cadre, la règle. On admire beaucoup la symétrie factice et la propreté imbécile. A l'hôpital de la marine, par exemple, les salles sont cirées de telle façon qu'un convalescent, essayant de marcher sur sa jambe remise, doit se casser l'autre en tombant.
(10) Mais c'est beau, ça brille, on s'y mire. Entre chaque salle est une cour, mais où le soleil ne vient jamais et dont soigneusement on arrache l'herbe. Les cuisines sont superbes, mais à une telle distance, qu'en hiver tout doit parvenir glacé aux malades. Il s'agit bien d'eux! Les
(15) casseroles ne sont-elles pas luisantes? Nous vîmes un homme qui s'était cassé le crâne en tombant d'une frégate et qui depuis dix-huit heures n'avait pas encore reçu de secours; mais ses draps étaient très blancs, car la lingerie est fort bien tenue.

(Gustave Flaubert, *Notes de voyage*, L'Intégrale)

81. "En tous lieux" signifie

 (A) nulle part
 (B) partout
 (C) ailleurs
 (D) quelque part

82. Le convalescent risque de se casser l'autre jambe parce que le sol est

 (A) mouillé
 (B) inégal
 (C) plein de trous
 (D) glissant

83. La cour entre chaque salle est

 (A) inondée de soleil
 (B) privée d'ombre
 (C) ensoleillée
 (D) privée de soleil

84. En hiver les repas sont servis aux malades

 (A) brûlants
 (B) tièdes
 (C) à point
 (D) très froids

85. Le ton de Flaubert dans ce passage est

 (A) sarcastique
 (B) sérieux
 (C) enjoué
 (D) tragique

S T O P

IF YOU FINISH BEFORE TIME IS CALLED, YOU MAY CHECK YOUR WORK ON THIS TEST ONLY.
DO NOT WORK ON ANY OTHER TEST IN THIS BOOK.

HOW TO SCORE THE PRINCETON REVIEW
FRENCH SUBJECT TEST

When you take the real exam, the proctors will collect your test booklet and bubble sheet and send your answer sheet to New Jersey where a computer looks at the pattern of filled-in ovals on your answer sheet and gives you a score. We are providing you, however, with this more primitive way of scoring your exam.

DETERMINING YOUR SCORE

STEP 1   Using the answers on the next page, determine how many questions you got right and how many you got wrong on the test. Remember, questions that you do not answer do not count as either right answers or wrong answers.

STEP 2   Write the number of correct answers on line A.   (A) _____

STEP 3   Write the number of wrong answers on line B. Divide   (B) _____ ÷ 3 = _____
that number by 3.

STEP 4   Subtract the number of wrong answers divided by 3 on line B from the number of correct answers on line A, and round to the nearest whole number. (C) is your **raw score.**   (A) _____ – (B) _____ = (C)

STEP 5   To determine your **real score,** look up your raw score in the left column of the Score Conversion Table on page 145; the corresponding score on the right is the score you made on the exam.

ANSWERS TO FRENCH SUBJECT TEST 2

Question number	Correct answer	Right	Wrong	Question number	Correct answer	Right	Wrong	Question number	Correct answer	Right	Wrong
1.	C	___	___	36.	C	___	___	71.	B	___	___
2.	D	___	___	37.	C	___	___	72.	D	___	___
3.	C	___	___	38.	B	___	___	73.	C	___	___
4.	B	___	___	39.	D	___	___	74.	B	___	___
5.	A	___	___	40.	A	___	___	75.	C	___	___
6.	D	___	___	41.	B	___	___	76.	C	___	___
7.	A	___	___	42.	D	___	___	77.	B	___	___
8.	B	___	___	43.	B	___	___	78.	A	___	___
9.	C	___	___	44.	C	___	___	79.	B	___	___
10.	D	___	___	45.	C	___	___	80.	D	___	___
11.	A	___	___	46.	D	___	___	81.	B	___	___
12.	A	___	___	47.	B	___	___	82.	D	___	___
13.	C	___	___	48.	C	___	___	83.	D	___	___
14.	A	___	___	49.	C	___	___	84.	D	___	___
15.	C	___	___	50.	A	___	___	85.	A	___	___
16.	A	___	___	51.	D	___	___				
17.	B	___	___	52.	D	___	___				
18.	C	___	___	53.	A	___	___				
19.	B	___	___	54.	B	___	___				
20.	D	___	___	55.	C	___	___				
21.	C	___	___	56.	B	___	___				
22.	B	___	___	57.	C	___	___				
23.	A	___	___	58.	D	___	___				
24.	B	___	___	59.	C	___	___				
25.	D	___	___	60.	A	___	___				
26.	A	___	___	61.	C	___	___				
27.	C	___	___	62.	C	___	___				
28.	B	___	___	63.	C	___	___				
29.	C	___	___	64.	A	___	___				
30.	C	___	___	65.	B	___	___				
31.	D	___	___	66.	A	___	___				
32.	A	___	___	67.	B	___	___				
33.	A	___	___	68.	D	___	___				
34.	B	___	___	69.	D	___	___				
35.	B	___	___	70.	A	___	___				

THE PRINCETON REVIEW FRENCH SUBJECT TEST
SCORE CONVERSION TABLE

Raw score	Scaled score	Raw score	Scaled score	Raw score	Scaled score
85	800	45	630	5	410
84	800	44	620	4	410
83	800	43	620	3	400
82	800	42	610	2	400
81	800	41	610	1	390
80	800	40	600	0	390
79	800	39	600	−1	380
78	800	38	590	−2	380
77	800	37	580	−3	370
76	790	36	580	−4	360
75	790	35	570	−5	360
74	780	34	570	−6	350
73	780	33	560	−7	350
72	770	32	560	−8	340
71	770	31	550	−9	340
70	760	30	550	−10	330
69	760	29	540	−11	330
68	750	28	540	−12	320
67	740	27	530	−13	320
66	740	26	530	−14	310
65	730	25	520	−15	300
64	730	24	520	−16	290
63	720	23	510	−17	290
62	720	22	500	−18	280
61	710	21	500	−19	280
60	710	20	490	−20	270
59	700	19	490	−21	270
58	700	18	480	−22	260
57	690	17	480	−23	260
56	690	16	470	−24	250
55	680	15	470	−25 through −28	240
54	680	14	460		
53	670	13	460		
52	660	12	450		
51	660	11	450		
50	650	10	440		
49	650	9	430		
48	640	8	430		
47	640	7	420		
46	630	6	420		

11

Practice SAT French Subject Test 2: Answers and Explanations

EXPLANATIONS

The possible choices are examined for clues that should have indicated the correct answer. To help explain why a choice is right or wrong, resemblances between English and French words are noted, grammatical explanations are given, and an analysis of the comprehension questions is provided. Key words in the English translations of the questions are in **bold face**, as are the correct answers.

Part A

1. He is . . . again. We are going to miss the train.

   Key phrase: *rater le train*
   fill in: late

   (A) early
   (B) on time
   (C) late
   (D) in agreement

2. Don't forget your umbrella; it's going to . . .
   tonight.

   Key word: *parapluie*
   Fill in: rain

   (A) cry—look-alike trap: *pleurer* (cry)/ *pleuvoir* (rain)
   (B) be cold
   (C) open
   (D) rain

3. There's nothing left in the refrigerator. I have to . . .

   Key phrase: *il n'y a plus rien*
   Fill in: go shopping

   (A) take a shower
   (B) mow the lawn
   (C) go shopping
   (D) set the table

4. I have a pain in my . . . . I'm going to make an
   appointment with the orthopedist.

   Key word: *orthopédiste*
   Fill in: knee

   (A) nose
   (B) knee
   (C) ears
   (D) physician

5. His car keeps breaking down and he is really . . .

   Key phrase: *est toujours en panne*
   Fill in: fed up

   (A) fed up
   (B) sea
   (C) honey
   (D) disgusted

6. At dusk the sky . . . with a thousand lights.

   Key phrase: *de mille feux*
   Fill in: sparkled

   (A) turned off
   (B) disappeared
   (C) fell
   (D) sparkled

7. He found the test he . . . yesterday very hard.

   Key word: *l'examen*
   Fill in: took

   (A) took – Watch out for this *faux ami*! *Passer un examen* means "to take an exam," while "to pass an exam" is *réussir un examen*.
   (B) took (in his hand)
   (C) caught
   (D) received

8. Jean is going to buy books at the . . .

   Key word: *acheter*
   Fill in: bookstore

   (A) butcher's
   (B) bookstore – Watch out for this *faux ami*! *Librairie* means "bookstore," while *bibliothèque* means "library."
   (C) pastry shop
   (D) library

9. She is so allergic to dust that she . . . repeatedly.

   Key word: *allergique*
   Fill in: sneezes

   (A) bursts
   (B) splashes
   (C) sneezes
   (D) hugs

10. He has done everything to reach his . . .

    Key word: *atteindre*
    Fill in: goal

    (A) test
    (B) work
    (C) branch
    (D) goal

11. He fainted when he heard . . .

    Key word: *apprenant*
    Fill in: the news

    (A) the news
    (B) the lesson
    (C) the armchair
    (D) the trash can

12. Nobody is answering the door; she is probably not . . .

    Key phrase: *personne ne répond*
    Fill in: there

    (A) there—"to be present" is *être là*
    (B) above
    (C) under
    (D) beside

13. The car . . . dead in front of the child who was running across the street.

    Key word: *voiture*
    Fill in: stopped

    (A) lost its temper
    (B) made sure
    (C) stopped
    (D) cried out

14. They have chosen to live . . . with their three young children.

    Key word: *habiter*
    Fill in: in the suburbs

    (A) in the suburbs
    (B) on the way
    (C) secretly
    (D) late

15. They are full of energy and are . . . every morning at 6.

    Key phrase: *Ils sont pleins d'énergie*
    Fill in: up

    (A) lying
    (B) sitting
    (C) up
    (D) angry

16. Not knowing what to do, I asked my lawyer for . . .

Key phrase: *ne sachant que faire*
Fill in: advice

(A) advice
(B) contribution
(C) contact
(D) company

17. For her interview with her future boss tomorrow, she is going to wear . . .

Key words: *elle va mettre*
Fill in: suit

(A) a shoe
(B) a woman's suit—*tailleur* is used for women, while *costume* is used for men
(C) a man's suit
(D) a hanger

18. She has . . . a lot of money to buy her house.

Key phrase: *beaucoup d'argent*
Fill in: borrowed

(A) lent
(B) knocked down
(C) borrowed
(D) sold

19. In order to make this cake, you . . . a lot of sugar.

Key phrase: *pour faire ce gâteau*
Fill in: need

(A) want
(B) need
(C) are thirsty
(D) are afraid

20. He is exhausted; he has worked . . .

Key phrase: *exténué*
Fill in: too much

(A) a little
(B) soon
(C) often
(D) too much

Part B

21. Pronouns

    (A) whose—*perdre* takes a direct object
    (B) to whom—*perdre* takes a direct object and a book is not a person
    (C) correct—which, right answer because *que* is a direct object pronoun
    (D) when it is not an interrogative pronoun, *lequel* can only be used with a preposition, i.e., *avec lequel, pour lequel*

22. Prepositions

    (A) at
    (B) correct—*pour*, here, means "in order to"
    (C) because
    (D) after

23. Verbs

    (A) correct—the infinitive is required when a verb follows another verb
    (B) past participle—grammatically incorrect
    (C) imperfect—grammatically incorrect
    (D) present participle—grammatically incorrect

24. Prepositions

    (A) *Danemark* is masculine; *de* in this case can only be used with a feminine country, i.e. *de France, de Belgique*
    (B) correct—*Danemark* is masculine
    (C) *en* could only work with a feminine country, i.e. *en France, en Suisse*
    (D) *aux* is plural—grammatically incorrect

25. Adverbs

    (A) the adverb *beaucoup* cannot be used before *bien*
    (B) the adverb *beaucoup* cannot be used before *meilleur*
    (C) makes no sense
    (D) correct—*mieux*, the comparative form of *bien*, may be preceded by *beaucoup*

26. Past Participles

    (A) correct—the verb *mettre* takes *avoir*, so the past participle agrees with the direct object *robe*, placed before the verb
    (B) grammatically incorrect—no past participle agreement
    (C) grammatically incorrect—no past participle agreement
    (D) grammatically incorrect—infinitive

27. Conjunctions

(A) although: followed by the subjunctive form of the verb
(B) before: followed by the subjunctive form of the verb
(C) correct—since, *puisque,* is followed by the indicative form of the verb
(D) unless: followed by the subjunctive form of the verb

28. Adverbs

(A) there
(B) correct—where
(C) towards
(D) near

29. Prepositions

(A) in
(B) during
(C) correct—before
(D) at

30. Subjunctive

(A) I was: imperfect—wrong tense
(B) I would be: conditional—wrong tense
(C) correct—subjunctive required after *bien que*
(D) I am: present—wrong tense

31. Pronouns

(A) makes no sense because *quelque* is not a pronoun
(B) little—makes no sense
(C) a little—*un peu* is used with something that is not numbered, i.e. *un peu de vin, de lait, de salade . . .* It would therefore be used after a question such as, *est-ce que tu veux du vin, du lait, de la salade . . . ?*
(D) correct—"one," *un* is used as a pronoun here.

32. Pronouns

(A) correct—*y* replaces *à la poste,* which is a place
(B) from there—*en* makes no sense with the verb *aller*; it can be used with *venir: j'en viens*
(C) always—makes no sense
(D) tomorrow—makes no sense

33. Conditional

(A) correct—"would win": present conditional is required after *si elle s'entraînait*
(B) won: imperfect—wrong tense
(C) will win: future—wrong tense
(D) has won: *passé composé*—wrong tense

34. Subjunctive

    (A) I went: imperfect—wrong tense
    (B) correct—subjunctive of the verb *aller* required after *il faut que*
    (C) I will go: future—wrong tense
    (D) I would go: conditional—wrong tense

Part C

35. Vocabulary

    (A) after—makes no sense
    (B) correct—since
    (C) for—makes no sense
    (D) in—*dans* is not used before *le matin*

36. Adjectives

    (A) all—would require the article *les*
    (B) each one—makes no sense
    (C) correct—every
    (D) some—makes no sense

37. Pronouns

    (A) grammatically wrong—*lui* is never a direct object
    (B) grammatically wrong—*la* refers to *elle*, not *il*
    (C) correct—*le* is masculine and a direct object
    (D) grammatically wrong—*leur* is indirect and plural

38. Pronouns

    (A) from there—*en* makes no sense here
    (B) correct—*y* refers to *les cafés*
    (C) in—makes no sense
    (D) where—makes no sense

39. Past Participles

    (A) grammatically wrong—masculine ending
    (B) grammatically wrong—infinitive
    (C) grammatically wrong—plural feminine ending
    (D) correct—refers to *la foule*, which is feminine and singular

40. Prepositions

    (A) correct—*s'adresser* takes *à* and means *parler à*
    (B) toward—inappropriate
    (C) with—makes no sense
    (D) for—makes no sense

41. Verbs

    (A) grammatically incorrect—past participle
    (B) correct—the infinitive is used after a preposition
    (C) grammatically incorrect—plural past participle
    (D) grammatically incorrect—imperfect

42. Prepositions

    (A) through—makes no sense
    (B) up to here—makes no sense
    (C) at the—makes no sense
    (D) correct—"to the end"; *bout* is a masculine noun and therefore needs the article *le*. *Jusqu'à* becomes *jusqu'au*—*jusqu'à* followed by a feminine noun would be *jusqu'à la* as in *jusqu'à la fin*.

43. Vocabulary

    (A) head
    (B) correct—back
    (C) ear
    (D) eyes

44. Vocabulary

    (A) pulling
    (B) carrying
    (C) correct—shrugging
    (D) passing

45. Prepositions

    (A) ------- *continuer* requires a preposition
    (B) for
    (C) correct—*continuer à*
    (D) in

46. Relative Pronouns

    (A) ------- in French you may not omit a relative pronoun or a conjunction such as "that" or "which" in English
    (B) literally, the which
    (C) whose—*dont* is wrong because *adresser* takes a direct object: *adresser une lettre*
    (D) correct—direct object relative pronoun

47. Verbs

    (A) subjunctive not needed here
    (B) correct—*adresser* takes *avoir* and the correct tense is the *passé composé* in the first person
    (C) will have—the future makes no sense here
    (D) had—*avait*, wrong tense, wrong person

48. Present Participles

    (A) wrong verb—need *être*, not *avoir*
    (B) before—makes no sense
    (C) correct—*rester* takes *être*
    (D) was—makes no sense in the context

49. Pronouns

    (A) wrong—a formal letter requires *vous*

    (B) me—this would refer back to the speaker

    (C) correct

    (D) him—there is no third party in the sentence

50. Prepositions

    (A) correct—the French expression is *prendre en considération*

    (B) with

    (C) by

    (D) as

51. Pronouns

    (A) wrong: *leur* is an indirect object pronoun, while *emmener* takes a direct object

    (B) wrong: *emmener* starts with a vowel

    (C) makes no sense because *emmener* is not a reflexive verb

    (D) correct—refers to the narrator: *emmener* starts with a vowel and the *m'* is required

52. Vocabulary

    (A) maybe

    (B) yet

    (C) once—wrong because of the imperfect

    (D) correct—often

53. Verbs

    (A) correct—French idiom, *venir de* + infinitive means to have just + past participle. *Je viens de manger*: "I have just eaten"

    (B) has come—*passé composé*

    (C) will come—future

    (D) wrong form—third person plural

54. Conjunctions

    (A) *qui* is a relative pronoun, never a conjunction, which is needed here

    (B) correct—"that": *que* is the correct conjunction here

    (C) since—makes no sense

    (D) as soon as—makes no sense

55. Vocabulary

    (A) demolished

    (B) built

    (C) correct

    (D) created

56. Prepositions

    (A) on

    (B) correct—with

    (C) by

    (D) like

Part D

57. When the autumn rain arrived, the grandmother was
    - (A) "edgy"
    - (B) "sad"
    - **(C) correct: "glad"**—*accueillait du même soupir soulagé la pluie d'automne*—the grandmother **"welcomed the autumn rain with the same sigh of relief"**
    - (D) "proud"

58. During the summer months, Jacques
    - (A) "worked a lot"—familiar words, wrong context
    - (B) "spent his time reading"—no mention of reading in the text
    - (C) "never stopped having fun"—on the contrary, the text refers to Jacques's *ennui*
    - **(D) correct: "did not know how to entertain himself"**—key words *piétinements d'ennui*

59. When she was a little girl, the grandmother
    - (A) "had shorter vacations than Jacques"—she had no vacation at all: *Je n'ai jamais eu de vacances, moi.*
    - (B) "used to draw pictures during her free time"—no context for this
    - **(C) correct: "spent all her time working"**—*elle avait travaillé enfant, et travaillé sans relâche.*
    - (D) "never did anything"—wrong: *elle avait travaillé sans relâche.*

60. According to the passage, we understand that
    - **(A) correct: "Jacques continues his studies"**—*lorsque Jacques entra en troisième*
    - (B) "the grandmother does not want Jacques to keep going to school"—*Elle admettait que, pour un bénéfice plus grand, son petit-fils pendant quelques années ne rapporte pas d'argent à la maison.*—"She agreed that for a greater benefit, her grandson would not bring home any money for a few years."
    - (C) "the grandmother is opposed to Jacques's having a summer job"—no, since she says *Tu vas travailler cet été.*
    - (D) "Jacques is the third in his class"—familiar words—wrong context

61. The grandmother wants Jacques to have a job so that he
    (A) "might have some pocket money"—no context for this
    (B) "might be able to pay for his studies"—no context for this
    (C) correct: "might contribute to the family expenses"—*rapporter un peu d'argent à la maison*—"bring home some money"
    (D) "might learn a trade"—no context for this

    ───────────────────────────────────

62. The three-year-old child is crying because
    (A) "he has lost his piece of chocolate"
    (B) "he has hurt himself"
    (C) correct: "he does not know where his family is"—*perdu*: lost
    (D) "it is dark"

63. The shutters of the store are
    (A) "open"
    (B) "up"
    (C) correct: *baissés*—"down"
    (D) "torn"

64. The woman "rushes to him" means that she goes toward the child
    (A) correct: "running"
    (B) "slowly"
    (C) "crying"
    (D) "unconcerned"

65. She "presses him tightly against her" means that she
    (A) "pushes him away"
    (B) correct: "hugs him"
    (C) "smiles at him"
    (D) "hits him"

66. Who does the woman think of as she carries the child away?
    (A) correct: "her own son"—*en pensant à l'enfant qu'on n'a pas retrouvé*
    (B) "the son of one of the refugees"
    (C) "the reader's son"
    (D) "the son of a guard"

67. The traffic jams mentioned in the text

    (A) "are used to cork a bottle"—double meaning of
        the word *bouchon*, either a cork or a traffic jam
    **(B) correct: "are traffic jams"—a street is
        embouteillée when it is jammed with cars**
    (C) "delay the trains"
    (D) "avoid wasting time"

68. According to the text, the combination Train + Car
    Rental

    (A) "is more expensive"
    (B) "is too expensive"
    (C) "is not very convenient"
    **(D) correct: "is a good deal"—*Tout en réalisant de
        vraies economies*!**

---

69. According to this article, the French

    (A) "go to the movies more and more often"
    (B) "seldom go to the movies"
    (C) "would rather watch television"
    **(D) correct: "enjoy watching movies at home more
        and more"—*Les Français auraient-ils attrapé le
        virus du home cinéma*? "Have the French caught
        the home-theater virus?"**

70. The equipments linked to the home theater

    **(A) correct: "have more and more success"—*2002
        devrait être l'année de l'explosion de ce marché
        en France*—"2002 should be the booming year
        of this market in France"**
    (B) "are a total failure"
    (C) "are not very interesting"
    (D) "are not in"—*être dans le vent* is a French idiom
        meaning *être à la mode*

71. Today, audiovisual equipment is

    (A) "more expensive"
    **(B) correct: "cheaper"—*la baisse des prix*: lower
        prices**
    (C) "exorbitant"—literally "out of price"
    (D) "prohibitive"—literally "that cannot be reached"

72. "The general public" represents

    (A) "a few privileged people"
    (B) "famous people"
    (C) "film enthusiasts"
    (D) correct: "most people"

73. ". . . the manufacturers have more and more affordable products at their disposal" means that they

(A) "are getting rid of them"
(B) "need them"
(C) correct: "have access to them"—watch out! *Disposer de* **here does not mean "to dispose of" but "to have at one's disposal."** i.e. *Je dispose de 1000 pour m'acheter un ordinateur* **means "I have 1000 euros at my disposal to buy a computer."**
(D) "make them"

---

74. When do you have to prepare the dough for the madeleines?

(A) "the next day"
(B) correct: "the day before"—*la veille*: **the day before**
(C) "two hours ahead of time"
(D) "yesterday"

75. According to the recipe, pastis is an ingredient which is

(A) "a must"
(B) "sweet"
(C) correct: "optional"—*facultatif*
(D) "fragrant"

---

76. "I have already hinted to you that" means "I have already"

(A) "told you"
(B) "repeated to you"
(C) correct: "suggested to you"
(D) "lied to you"

77. The hunchback has "big plans" because

(A) "he needs money right away"
(B) correct: "he thinks about his daughter's future"—*Je dois assurer l'avenir de ma fillette*: **"I have to secure my little girl's future."**
(C) "he is a philosopher"
(D) "he loves money"

78. From the hunchback's speech, Ugolin remembers

(A) correct: "only the last words"—*De ce discours, Ugolin ne retint que les derniers mots. Ne . . . que* **means "only."**
(B) "maybe the first words"
(C) "always the last sentence"
(D) "everything but the end"

79. In lines 19–23, upon hearing the hunchback's plans, Ugolin is

   (A) "amused"
   (B) correct: "very worried"
   (C) "full of joy"
   (D) "reassured"

80. Ugolin is trying to find out whether the hunchback

   (A) "is going to plant a vineyard"
   (B) "will save the olive trees and the almond trees"
   (C) "is planning to sell thistles"
   (D) correct: "knows about the existence of the spring"—*il connaissait donc la source*: "so he knew about the spring."

81. "In every place" means

   (A) "nowhere"
   (B) correct: "everywhere"
   (C) "somewhere else"
   (D) "somewhere"

82. The convalescent runs the risk of breaking his other leg because the floor is

   (A) "wet"
   (B) "uneven"
   (C) "full of holes"
   (D) correct: "slippery"—*les salles sont cirées de telle façon qu'un convalescent, . . . doit se casser l'autre en tombant*—"the rooms are waxed in such a way that a convalescent . . . must fall and break the other one"

83. The courtyard in between every room is

   (A) "full of sun"
   (B) "without any shade"
   (C) "sunny"
   (D) correct: "without any sun"—*mais où le soleil ne vient jamais*: "but where the sun never comes"

84. In winter the patients' meals are

   (A) "piping hot"
   (B) "lukewarm"
   (C) "at the right temperature"
   (D) correct: "very cold"—*tout doit parvenir glacé*: icy cold

85. Flaubert's tone in this passage is

   (A) correct: "sarcastic"—Flaubert describes what he calls *la symétrie factice* ("the artificial symmetry") and *la propreté imbécile* ("the stupid cleanliness") of the arsenal
   (B) "serious"
   (C) "playful"
   (D) "tragic"

ABOUT THE AUTHORS

Monique Gaden, a graduate of the Université de Lyon, and Simone Ingram, a graduate of the Université de Lille, have taught French and English for many years. They have collaborated on the revision of this book and on the creation of the second practice test.

Practice Test 1 Form

Completely darken bubbles with a No. 2 pencil. If you make a mistake, be sure to erase mark completely. Erase all stray marks.

Section 1

1. A B C D E	26. A B C D E	51. A B C D E	76. A B C D E
2. A B C D E	27. A B C D E	52. A B C D E	77. A B C D E
3. A B C D E	28. A B C D E	53. A B C D E	78. A B C D E
4. A B C D E	29. A B C D E	54. A B C D E	79. A B C D E
5. A B C D E	30. A B C D E	55. A B C D E	80. A B C D E
6. A B C D E	31. A B C D E	56. A B C D E	81. A B C D E
7. A B C D E	32. A B C D E	57. A B C D E	82. A B C D E
8. A B C D E	33. A B C D E	58. A B C D E	83. A B C D E
9. A B C D E	34. A B C D E	59. A B C D E	84. A B C D E
10. A B C D E	35. A B C D E	60. A B C D E	85. A B C D E
11. A B C D E	36. A B C D E	61. A B C D E	
12. A B C D E	37. A B C D E	62. A B C D E	
13. A B C D E	38. A B C D E	63. A B C D E	
14. A B C D E	39. A B C D E	64. A B C D E	
15. A B C D E	40. A B C D E	65. A B C D E	
16. A B C D E	41. A B C D E	66. A B C D E	
17. A B C D E	42. A B C D E	67. A B C D E	
18. A B C D E	43. A B C D E	68. A B C D E	
19. A B C D E	44. A B C D E	69. A B C D E	
20. A B C D E	45. A B C D E	70. A B C D E	
21. A B C D E	46. A B C D E	71. A B C D E	
22. A B C D E	47. A B C D E	72. A B C D E	
23. A B C D E	48. A B C D E	73. A B C D E	
24. A B C D E	49. A B C D E	74. A B C D E	
25. A B C D E	50. A B C D E	75. A B C D E	

Practice Test 2 Form

Completely darken bubbles with a No. 2 pencil. If you make a mistake, be sure to erase mark completely. Erase all stray marks.

Section 2

1. Ⓐ Ⓑ Ⓒ Ⓓ Ⓔ	26. Ⓐ Ⓑ Ⓒ Ⓓ Ⓔ	51. Ⓐ Ⓑ Ⓒ Ⓓ Ⓔ	76. Ⓐ Ⓑ Ⓒ Ⓓ Ⓔ
2. Ⓐ Ⓑ Ⓒ Ⓓ Ⓔ	27. Ⓐ Ⓑ Ⓒ Ⓓ Ⓔ	52. Ⓐ Ⓑ Ⓒ Ⓓ Ⓔ	77. Ⓐ Ⓑ Ⓒ Ⓓ Ⓔ
3. Ⓐ Ⓑ Ⓒ Ⓓ Ⓔ	28. Ⓐ Ⓑ Ⓒ Ⓓ Ⓔ	53. Ⓐ Ⓑ Ⓒ Ⓓ Ⓔ	78. Ⓐ Ⓑ Ⓒ Ⓓ Ⓔ
4. Ⓐ Ⓑ Ⓒ Ⓓ Ⓔ	29. Ⓐ Ⓑ Ⓒ Ⓓ Ⓔ	54. Ⓐ Ⓑ Ⓒ Ⓓ Ⓔ	79. Ⓐ Ⓑ Ⓒ Ⓓ Ⓔ
5. Ⓐ Ⓑ Ⓒ Ⓓ Ⓔ	30. Ⓐ Ⓑ Ⓒ Ⓓ Ⓔ	55. Ⓐ Ⓑ Ⓒ Ⓓ Ⓔ	80. Ⓐ Ⓑ Ⓒ Ⓓ Ⓔ
6. Ⓐ Ⓑ Ⓒ Ⓓ Ⓔ	31. Ⓐ Ⓑ Ⓒ Ⓓ Ⓔ	56. Ⓐ Ⓑ Ⓒ Ⓓ Ⓔ	81. Ⓐ Ⓑ Ⓒ Ⓓ Ⓔ
7. Ⓐ Ⓑ Ⓒ Ⓓ Ⓔ	32. Ⓐ Ⓑ Ⓒ Ⓓ Ⓔ	57. Ⓐ Ⓑ Ⓒ Ⓓ Ⓔ	82. Ⓐ Ⓑ Ⓒ Ⓓ Ⓔ
8. Ⓐ Ⓑ Ⓒ Ⓓ Ⓔ	33. Ⓐ Ⓑ Ⓒ Ⓓ Ⓔ	58. Ⓐ Ⓑ Ⓒ Ⓓ Ⓔ	83. Ⓐ Ⓑ Ⓒ Ⓓ Ⓔ
9. Ⓐ Ⓑ Ⓒ Ⓓ Ⓔ	34. Ⓐ Ⓑ Ⓒ Ⓓ Ⓔ	59. Ⓐ Ⓑ Ⓒ Ⓓ Ⓔ	84. Ⓐ Ⓑ Ⓒ Ⓓ Ⓔ
10. Ⓐ Ⓑ Ⓒ Ⓓ Ⓔ	35. Ⓐ Ⓑ Ⓒ Ⓓ Ⓔ	60. Ⓐ Ⓑ Ⓒ Ⓓ Ⓔ	85. Ⓐ Ⓑ Ⓒ Ⓓ Ⓔ
11. Ⓐ Ⓑ Ⓒ Ⓓ Ⓔ	36. Ⓐ Ⓑ Ⓒ Ⓓ Ⓔ	61. Ⓐ Ⓑ Ⓒ Ⓓ Ⓔ	
12. Ⓐ Ⓑ Ⓒ Ⓓ Ⓔ	37. Ⓐ Ⓑ Ⓒ Ⓓ Ⓔ	62. Ⓐ Ⓑ Ⓒ Ⓓ Ⓔ	
13. Ⓐ Ⓑ Ⓒ Ⓓ Ⓔ	38. Ⓐ Ⓑ Ⓒ Ⓓ Ⓔ	63. Ⓐ Ⓑ Ⓒ Ⓓ Ⓔ	
14. Ⓐ Ⓑ Ⓒ Ⓓ Ⓔ	39. Ⓐ Ⓑ Ⓒ Ⓓ Ⓔ	64. Ⓐ Ⓑ Ⓒ Ⓓ Ⓔ	
15. Ⓐ Ⓑ Ⓒ Ⓓ Ⓔ	40. Ⓐ Ⓑ Ⓒ Ⓓ Ⓔ	65. Ⓐ Ⓑ Ⓒ Ⓓ Ⓔ	
16. Ⓐ Ⓑ Ⓒ Ⓓ Ⓔ	41. Ⓐ Ⓑ Ⓒ Ⓓ Ⓔ	66. Ⓐ Ⓑ Ⓒ Ⓓ Ⓔ	
17. Ⓐ Ⓑ Ⓒ Ⓓ Ⓔ	42. Ⓐ Ⓑ Ⓒ Ⓓ Ⓔ	67. Ⓐ Ⓑ Ⓒ Ⓓ Ⓔ	
18. Ⓐ Ⓑ Ⓒ Ⓓ Ⓔ	43. Ⓐ Ⓑ Ⓒ Ⓓ Ⓔ	68. Ⓐ Ⓑ Ⓒ Ⓓ Ⓔ	
19. Ⓐ Ⓑ Ⓒ Ⓓ Ⓔ	44. Ⓐ Ⓑ Ⓒ Ⓓ Ⓔ	69. Ⓐ Ⓑ Ⓒ Ⓓ Ⓔ	
20. Ⓐ Ⓑ Ⓒ Ⓓ Ⓔ	45. Ⓐ Ⓑ Ⓒ Ⓓ Ⓔ	70. Ⓐ Ⓑ Ⓒ Ⓓ Ⓔ	
21. Ⓐ Ⓑ Ⓒ Ⓓ Ⓔ	46. Ⓐ Ⓑ Ⓒ Ⓓ Ⓔ	71. Ⓐ Ⓑ Ⓒ Ⓓ Ⓔ	
22. Ⓐ Ⓑ Ⓒ Ⓓ Ⓔ	47. Ⓐ Ⓑ Ⓒ Ⓓ Ⓔ	72. Ⓐ Ⓑ Ⓒ Ⓓ Ⓔ	
23. Ⓐ Ⓑ Ⓒ Ⓓ Ⓔ	48. Ⓐ Ⓑ Ⓒ Ⓓ Ⓔ	73. Ⓐ Ⓑ Ⓒ Ⓓ Ⓔ	
24. Ⓐ Ⓑ Ⓒ Ⓓ Ⓔ	49. Ⓐ Ⓑ Ⓒ Ⓓ Ⓔ	74. Ⓐ Ⓑ Ⓒ Ⓓ Ⓔ	
25. Ⓐ Ⓑ Ⓒ Ⓓ Ⓔ	50. Ⓐ Ⓑ Ⓒ Ⓓ Ⓔ	75. Ⓐ Ⓑ Ⓒ Ⓓ Ⓔ	

NOTES

NOTES

NOTES

NOTES

NOTES

NOTES

NOTES

NOTES

NOTES

AP Exams

Cracking the AP — Biology,
2004–2005 Edition
0-375-76393-7 • $18.00

Cracking the AP — Calculus AB & BC,
2004–2005 Edition
0-375-76381-3 • $19.00

Cracking the AP — Chemistry,
2004–2005 Edition
0-375-76382-1• $18.00

Cracking the AP — Computer Science AB & BC, 2004-2005 Edition
0-375-76383-X • $19.00

Cracking the AP — Economics (Macro & Micro), 2004-2005 Edition
0-375-76384-8 • $18.00

Cracking the AP — English Literature,
2004–2005 Edition
0-375-76385-6 • $18.00

Cracking the AP — European History,
2004–2005 Edition
0-375-76386-4 • $18.00

Cracking the AP — Physics B & C,
2004–2005 Edition
0-375-76387-2 • $19.00

Cracking the AP — Psychology,
2004–2005 Edition
0-375-76388-0 • $18.00

Cracking the AP — Spanish,
2004–2005 Edition
0-375-76389-9 • $18.00

Cracking the AP — Statistics,
2004–2005 Edition
0-375-76390-2 • $19.00

Cracking the AP — U.S. Government and Politics, 2004–2005 Edition
0-375-76391-0 • $18.00

Cracking the AP — U.S. History,
2004–2005 Edition
0-375-76392-9 • $18.00

Cracking the AP — World History,
2004–2005 Edition
0-375-76380-5 • $18.00

SAT Subject Tests

Cracking the SAT: Biology E/M Subject Test,
2005-2006 Edition
0-375-76447-X • $19.00

Cracking the SAT: Chemistry Subject Test,
2005-2006 Edition
0-375-76448-8 • $18.00

Cracking the SAT: French Subject Test,
2005-2006 Edition
0-375-76449-6 • $18.00

Cracking the SAT: Literature Subject Test,
2005-2006 Edition
0-375-76446-1 • $18.00

Cracking the SAT: Math Subject Tests,
2005-2006 Edition
0-375-76451-8 • $19.00

Cracking the SAT: Physics Subject Test,
2005-2006 Edition
0-375-76452-6 • $19.00

Cracking the SAT: Spanish Subject Test,
2005-2006 Edition
0-375-76453-4 • $18.00

Cracking the SAT: U.S. & World History Subject Tests, 2005-2006 Edition
0-375-76450-X • $19.00

Available at Bookstores Everywhere
PrincetonReview.com

Besoin de plus?

If you want to learn more about how to excel on the SAT Subject Test in French, you're in the right place. Our expertise extends far beyond just this test. But this isn't about us, it's about getting you into the college of your choice.

One way to increase the number of fat envelopes you receive is to have strong test scores. So, if you're still nervous—relax. Consider all of your options.

We consistently improve students' scores through our books, classroom courses, private tutoring and online courses. Call 800-2Review or visit *PrincetonReview.com*.

If you like our *Cracking the SAT French Subject Test*, check out:
- *The Best 357 Colleges*
- *Cracking the New SAT*
- *11 Practice Tests for the New SAT and PSAT*
- *Cracking the SAT U.S. & World History Subject Tests*